*Dear Mann
God ble
journey in teaching
All God's children.
yours in Christ,*

CAREGIVER

A Journal of Hope Through Suffering

DEACON SEAN W. DOOLEY

xulon PRESS

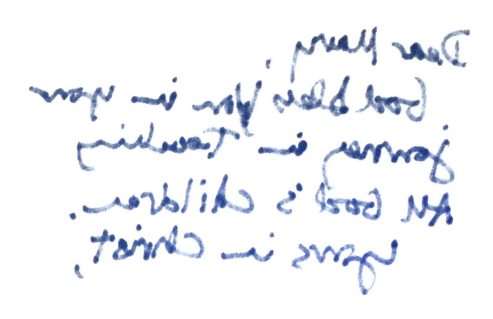

CAREGIVER
A Journal of Hope Through Suffering
by Deacon Sean W. Dooley

Printed in the United States of America.

ISBN 9781498433327

www.xulonpress.com

Table of Contents

This is Devoted to my wife; Kathi Dooley, my daughter; Erin Dooley, my mother-in-law; Henrietta Redepenning, mi compadre; Patricio Elizondo, Jr., my grandfather; William S. Wallace and my mother Helen Wanda (nee Wallace) Dooley for showing me how to care for others.

This is also dedicated to all the nameless Caregivers around the world and the professional Caregivers: the doctors, nurses, specialists and staff; who provide care and support for your loved ones.

I would like to send up a prayer of thanksgiving, praise and adoration to God for the Gift of life.

I want to thank all those prayer warriors who supported Kathi and me, with their spiritual as well as their physical presence, during our darkest hour. The Power of Prayer works!

ACRONYMS

http://www.mainlinehealth.org/doc/Page.asp?PageID=DOC000663

https://www.hanys.org/communications/publications/2008/2008_
health_care_acronyms.pdf

CCU – Cardiac Care Unit

CFM – Close Fitting Mask

CHF – Congestive Heart Failure

CM – Case Manager

CPR – Cardiopulmonary Resuscitation

CT – Computed Tomography (Scan)

CVOR – Cardiovascular Operating Room

DNR – Do Not Resuscitate Order

ECG – Electrocardiography

ED – Emergency Department (Emergency Room)

EHR – Electronic Health Record

EMR – Electronic Medical Record

EMS – Emergency Medical Services

EMT – Emergency Medical Technician

EOB – Explanation of Benefits

GP – General Practitioner

HIPAA – Health Insurance Portability & Accountability Act of 1996

HMO – Health Maintenance Organization

ICU – Intensive Care Unit

ID – Infectious Diseases

IM – Internal Medicine

INR – International Normalized Ratio

LTAC – Long Term Acute Care Facility

LTC – Long-Term Care

LVN – Licensed Vocational Nurse

MI – Myocardial Infarction (heart attack; a.k.a. acute myocardial infarction or AMI)

MRI – Magnetic Resonance Imaging

MRN – Medical Record Number

OT – occupational therapy

PA – Physician's Assistant

PCP – Primary Care Physician

PM&R – Physical Medicine and Rehabilitation

PM&R – Physical Medicine and Rehabilitation

PRN – As required or necessary

PT – Physical Therapy

Px – Prognosis

R.R. – Respiratory Rate

R.S.R. – Regular Sinus Rhythm

RT – Respiratory Therapy

Rx – Prescription

SFN – Superfibronectin

SICU – Surgical Intensive Care Unit

ST – Speech Therapy

1. PROLOGUE

The premise for these pages was predicated on one caregiver's perspective relative to the care and well-being of a loved one; over a 144 month period, these pages focus on the last 8 months. The basis is reinforced through caregiving experiences for the author before and after this timeframe. When did the end begin? When we were born? When was the end programmed? On our meeting? To what purpose does either end signify for those left behind (not to be confused with those who believe in the rapture)? What really are we to do with ourselves upon losing half of our being? How do we cope? How do we continue to awake day after day? What do we impart to others, who are in similar situations? Do we as former caregivers, serve as the Platos[1] for the next round of caregivers? The elders, if you will, of accommodating those wishing to know why their loved one was chosen to suffer and you as caregiver along with him/her in a different, yet just as permanent way? There may be support or therapy groups for these unknown servants, but there does not appear to be a Caregiver's Manual.

It is in these pages, I hope to present a compassionate outlook, based on my own personal and very recent experience. This is written from the perspective of someone who is blessed to have health insurance. The dichotomy of the relationship between health insurance, the healthcare industry and the patient is fodder for another tome. I am compelled to share these experiences, not that there is anything earth-shattering, or answers to the question, but more perhaps to be able to guide one who is currently living this experience and is alone in a city or town without a support network of close faith, family or friends.

I do not know if this is or will be considered a how to, guide, instruction manual or cookbook. Today it does not have the feel of structure, more of a personal journal freeform in style. This is my best forte as a generalist by nature, design and default. This kind of struck me while I'm sitting at home listening to Christmas playlist on my iPod. I started out listening to the local radio station; but it seems they're only playing the same twenty songs with twenty-five versions of "Jingle Bell Rock" and "Rockin' Around the Christmas Tree", not my brand of Christmas music. Granted the chants have put me in a reflective mood, a good thing for a self-professed 'writer'.

I'm up to 80 pages so far in this format with much more in other journals/logs/notes captured during this tragedy, which seemingly is headed toward a glorious ending that is yet to be determined. I do not know that the number of pages is as important as the message, which is what I'm hoping to impart. I am so blessed to have lived through two similar occasions in my life and shared with my wife Kathi. How will this benefit those who experience a less fortunate outcome?

My thoughts wander quite a bit, however this writing became a mission during my wife's darkest period of her life and mine. I pray the words of this writing will help someone. Someone who may be alone in their suffering struggle as Caregiver. What is contained herein is a personal journey of love, devotion and adoration for the angel God gave me.

We are blessed to receive the gift of Life, we should be thankful for every breath we take and not take any of this life for granted. How can you even feel you are entitled to it? You were nothing, would be nothing, if you had not been born and why, oh, why would you even consider anything so unthinkable as to give that Gift back? How can you even think you wish you were never born? What if you were not born? What would you feel then? Good, bad or indifferent; you would not.

Writing a bunch of prattle and filling up white space. Why? Because it's there and I can. From ICU Room # 408. October 9, 2014.

2. Introduction

Job spoke, saying:

Is not man's life on earth a drudgery?

Are not his days those of hirelings?

He is a slave who longs for the shade,

a hireling who waits for his wages.

So I have been assigned months of misery,

and troubled nights have been allotted to me.

If in bed I say, "When shall I arise?"

then the night drags on;

I am filled with restlessness until the dawn.

My days are swifter than a weaver's shuttle;

they come to an end without hope.

Remember that my life is like the wind;

I shall not see happiness again.²

T his may eventually be filed under Holiness in Suffering, but what
I'm musing about is the suffering of a caregiver. From what I

understand, this is a fairly recent recognized phenomenon. The position of the caregiver as a sufferer. You suffer witnessing a loved one suffer and you are unable to provide comfort or expertise and your only input to the care of your loved one is your presence, prayers and health insurance.

You cry when your loved one does not understand why she has been blessed with this malady, predicament, illness or misfortune. You, on the other hand seem to be blessed with fairly good health and well-being. Your spouse, sees your health and wonders aloud why that is so. As a caregiver, in your silent attention to your spouse/ward, you maintain your emotions, composure (most times) and serve in your presence as the rock and/or shoulder that your loved one and other family members and friends can lean on, during this time of need.

You spend hours praying and crying in the silence and stillness of the early morning and late night beseeching God for healing and peace for your loved one, carefully wording your wordless prayer. You still want her physically with you at the end of this current ordeal. You just cannot see yourself without her and you do not know why either, questioning the weakness of your own faith and what strikes to dismantle your beliefs. The devil is truly toying with you as the master of this world, while the Master of all appears at times, silent and aloof. Sometimes you feel like Job, then as penance for feeling that way or making that comment to someone else, you actually read the book of

Job and realize you are far from his suffering. But, I do not have to lose my whole family to feel devastated.

For my yoke is easy and my burden light[3]. This is what you attempt to impart to your loved ones, as well as your loved one. Your loved one should not be worrying about anything but their recovery and recuperation; you have 'everything' under control and in control. All the bills are being paid, the grass is cut, plants are watered, trash is being disposed of, her car is current with inspection and registration and oil change, clothes and dishes are washed, with food in the refrigerator, but the underlying issue is the empty home without her.

What about those grandchildren, who do not belong in the ICU? What do you tell them, that Gaga is very sick and you don't know when she is coming home (and in your heart, you do not believe that she is – O, ye of little faith).

How did this come to be? When you met, you were oh, so very young and the world was innocent and bountiful and yours for the asking. You thought you had all the answers, your eyes and hearts were filled with the wonderment of creation. The questions were never asked, the prayers never lifted up, we were going to live forever in each other under the eyes of God.

What do you tell your loved one when she asks; "Am I in hell?" or "Am I dying?" or tells you by writing "I want to live!".

There is something I want to communicate in these pages.

3. Your Loved One

25 Husbands, love your wives, even as Christ loved the church and handed himself over for her 26 to sanctify her, cleansing her by the bath of water with the word,

27 that he might present to himself the church in splendor, without spot or wrinkle or any such thing, that she might be holy and without blemish.

28 So [also] husbands should love their wives as their own bodies. He who loves his wife loves himself.

29 For no one hates his own flesh but rather nourishes and cherishes it, even as Christ does the church,

30 because we are members of his body.

31 "For this reason a man shall leave [his] father and [his] mother and be joined to his wife, and the two shall become one flesh."

32 This is a great mystery, but I speak in reference to Christ and the church.[4]

I begin this chapter with a verse reminding us of our marriage vows; for those of us who are married and those who may be considering the Sacrament of Matrimony.

"...for your lawful wife, to have and to hold, from this day forward, for better, for worse, for richer, for poorer, in sickness and in health, until death do you part?".[5] It is with these vows in my heart, that I wish to provide an introduction to the main or lead character of this story.

I met my future trophy wife, Kathi in September of 1971 in Biloxi, Mississippi, where I was stationed as an aircraft mechanic at Keesler AFB. I was introduced or rather she was introduced to me, by a friend of mine who brought her to my apartment on a date to attend a party at my 'pad'. My friend wanted to introduce her to a 'cool' guy, yes I was a legend in my own mind. Kathi was new to the neighborhood, more parties ensued and she would show up with yet other friends on dates to my place. What attracted me to her first (call me Shallow Hal), was of course her physical beauty, which was surpassed by her internal beauty once I got to know her and there was not an ounce of conceit within her; although, this tall, leggy blonde from Texas could have gotten away with thinking of herself only. Then, to top it off, she was able to say what she was thinking, most times without a filter. And to me, an introvert, this definitely added to the attraction and mystery of wanting to know this girl better. This country boy was taken aback by this whirlwind who was about to enter my life, permanently.

The beginning of the end for me occurred at the fourth party at my place and back then, my place was always open for a party. It was not just my place, I shared the apartment with a good friend. People would just show up and away we go. I was sitting on a couch with my then girlfriend, when Kathi came in and sat on my lap, with her back to my girlfriend, asking me if I had seen an earring she thought she might have lost in my apartment. This event led to several phone calls to her place (she lived in a dormitory) and agreements to meet. I did not have a landline in our apartment and this was way before cell phones, so I would call her number from a nearby pay phone.

The ensuing days led to weeks, and I first asked her to marry me in early November 1971, setting a date of February 5, 1972. We had no clue or plan, love at first sight does not allow for that, as we knew we were meant to be together. Kathi began talking about the beautiful babies we would have together. By the way, the first guy who brought her to my apartment was no longer my friend!

As Christmas approached and I was going 'home' to Iowa for Christmas and Kathi to her family at Andrews AFB in Maryland; I got cold feet and cancelled the wedding 'plans', telling Kathi not to come back. Looking back, this was my modus operandi, I usually 'broke up' with girlfriends around Christmas time and used it as a half-joke, so I would not have to buy presents and at that time, I was only receiving $34 take-home pay every two weeks. We had only recently received a substantial pay increase in November, bumping up my take home by nearly a $100 every two weeks and I was not quite used to that yet. There was probably a deeper reason for my wanting to be alone during the holidays, but I am not qualified to investigate. I'll leave that to the psychologists and psychiatrists and is not the focus of this book.

I returned to Biloxi after the Christmas holidays, in early January 1972. I was at a watering hole outside Gate # 2 called Your Place, on Howard Avenue, playing the pinball machine with a friend of mine who we all called 'Chuck'; a nickname, not even close to his real name. I was deep in battle with the machine, when I could hear Chuck, chortling behind me. He continued his laughing until the ball dropped behind the flippers and I looked up in the direction of his stare through the window and there was Kathi getting ready to walk in, that was it, I was lost in love.

Kathi and I were married in November 1972 by a base Chaplain who was a Catholic Priest; Fr. William O'Cleary in base chapel # 2 on Keesler. This was an event in and of itself.

I have to tell you how our 'wedding' came together. We made an appointment with the local Justice of the Peace (JP) for a Saturday wedding; I believe it was around 1:00 pm, because I had to march in a scheduled parade that morning. We and our entourage show up at a locked courthouse. I call the JP's house and his wife tells me that the JP is gone hunting for the week-end. What now??? One of our friends placed a call to the base chapel Officer on Duty (OD), explained the situation and was able to get the chaplain on duty to agree to marry us. We go to the base chapel at about 2:30 for a 3:00 P.M. wedding. While waiting, the choir was getting ready to practice and the organist approached us and asked us if we minded their 'playing' during our wedding. Are you kidding? We could not have planned this any better. Then we met the Chaplain, he was a Catholic Priest.

I had orders for Osan AFB in Korea, so I began my obligatory 30 day leave. We drove from Mississippi to Cedar Rapids to visit my folks first. Neither one of us had met our parents yet. It was 80° when we left Biloxi; it was 8° and going down, when we arrived in Cedar Rapids later that night. My 1964 Belair Station wagon died and my new wife almost did. While visiting my parents; Kathi became stricken with a type of virus which inflamed the protective layer around her Heart, a condition called Pericarditis. She went into the hospital in Cedar Rapids for three weeks. On December 26, 1972, the doctors agreed to release her if we promised to go to the hospital as soon as we got to Andrews AFB; where Kathi's parents were stationed. During this time, I had to borrow money from the Red Cross to fix my car. Fortunately, we did have a station wagon. Kathi slept in the back, while I set a land speed record as I made it to Kathi's parents' house (on base) in 17 hours. You have to picture this, I've never met Kathi's parents, I show up at 3:00 AM on their doorstep with their deathly ill daughter and I'm not groomed in accordance with AFR 35-10 (military grooming regulations); I have an afro (when I had hair and lots of it!) and a beard. This is where I received an instant lesson in 'family'. Welcome in/home,

23

hugs and breakfast. We finished breakfast and then drove to one of her parents' friend's house that were on vacation. Later that morning, as promised, I took her to the hospital at Andrews AFB, she was admitted within 15 minutes. Her liver and spleen were swollen and her Heart was swollen to twice it's normal size. They did not know if she was going to make it. I was to report to San Francisco on Jan 7, 1973, but the doctors said "you are not going anywhere". Kathi was in the hospital about 45 days.

My new father-n-law helped me apply for and I received a humanitarian reassignment to Andrews. During this time, I was living with my new in-laws, it gave us time to become acquainted, I also got to go to Church with them. One day, as my father-in-law was chauffeuring me between the various required offices, he told me how much he loved his daughter and reached over and patted me on the knee and said "Welcome to the Family".

When I separated from the USAF on April 4, 1974, I received much grief from my parents as well as Kathi's. However, I had made up my mind and Kathi and I were going to settle in the City of Love, New Orleans. A funny thing happened during those two months of vacation as we drove across the country visiting family and friends.

Our last stop before going to the final destination was the town where Kathi's mom was from and where my mother-in-law's six sisters and their families lived. We stayed here a week; which had a lasting impression on my life, I truly believe that Kathi is related to about 75%

of San Antonio and I met all of them during that week in the spring of 1974. What a family! Sixth and seventh cousins of this 'good' Catholic family are part of the inner circle; we rent Mesquite Hall for family Christmas. Kathi and I left for New Orleans and stayed a week. I had a job at the Pascagoula shipyard as an underwater welder trainee. One evening while staying at a friend's house, I stood up and asked Kathi if she wanted to live in San Antonio – we practically ran out of that trailer. We left the next morning and never looked back. It's just as well; I do not swim very well.

We began by settling in San Antonio, staying with one of Kathi's aunts and uncles for 30 days in May 1974 and I began working at Kelly AFB on June 4, as a civilian, pretty much for the same employer, I had 'left' two months earlier. We began our life on the Southsiiide! at the Utopia apartments. We were blessed almost nine months later on Feb 25, when our daughter Erin was born at the Nix downtown, where we were serenaded by "Bongo Joe", even though we were on the 21st floor! We bought our first house in June 1975 on Kate Schenck. As Erin began to grow, it was evident that we needed to find a 'younger' neighborhood. Most of the 'kids' in our neighborhood were our age. We found a house in Converse and moved there when Erin was two years old. This was a younger neighborhood that also included military families since we lived near Randolph AFB. Erin had many friends in this new neighborhood.

We were living on Bridget in Converse, when our son Ian blessed us on December 23, 1979, who the nurses dubbed "Mr. Personality", coming home in a Christmas stocking. Over the course of the next forty-one years in Converse and San Antonio, our marriage experienced some significant events, difficulties, challenges, highs, lows and almost ended on three occasions. But, it was also buoyed and held afloat by our children (family), dreams, perseverance and God's love and guidance (this was a later phenomenon in our adult lives). Some days were rocks, some were roses. The rocks threatened to sink us and the roses provided the safety net. Our safety net has been Jesus, His Church and our Faith-based family.

We celebrated our 35th Anniversary with renewal of our vows and a wedding Mass at St. Monica on Nov 17, 2007, with 200 of our closest friends and family.

Kathi has been the rock in terms of our family's faith foundation throughout our courtship and marriage and she has helped me to strengthen and deepen my faith to where I am today. Kathi and Father Pat have said they created a monster in me. Kathi has been a nurturing force even when we were experiencing difficulties as a wife and husband.

Other than our foolish behavior earlier in our marriage, we have experienced other challenges as parents and partners. It has been the faith taught to me by Kathi and her family, which enables us to meet the challenges head-on and get through them. God will get you through it.

Kathi has taught me about unconditional Love, this is how she loves. She gets hurt when others do not accept or reject that love. She lives the love Jesus taught us. This is how she approaches others.

She was the 'cool' mom to our children's friends. Kathi is loved back, by most everyone who meets her. She welcomes all with her bigger than life heart and it seems there is always room for one more in her heart. She is not cynical about life and has enjoyed what life offers and because her heart is open, she does sometimes get disappointed when her expectations are not met or does not meet her expectations.

Kathi was there for every one of our children's events as they grew. She was the atypical soccer mom and in charge of ensuring homework was accomplished. She was a girl scout leader for our daughter, while I was boy scout leader for my son, soccer coach for my daughter and son, rounding out baseball and basketball coach for my son . Kathi attended the scouts' events, whether it was the pinewood derby or a girl scout camp out and all school events. She continues that today with our grandchildren, as we are blessed to have them live nearby. Kathi ensures the family is represented at drama, dance, class recitals, school plays and served as soccer grandma, until the doctors told her not to drive while they figured out her diagnosis. Kathi was named 'Gaga' by our first granddaughter, before there was a Lady Gaga. Kathi had wanted to her grandchildren to call her Gommie after her grandmother, who Kathi had named and the tradition continues. I adopted pawpaw from Kathi's grandfather, who she also named and he was my sponsor into the Catholic church in 1992.

Fourteen years ago, Kathi began having trouble catching her breath. She went to several specialists and finally, a cardiologist discovered she was experiencing problems associated with a congenital heart defect, or Atrial Septum Defect (ASD). She was born with a hole in her heart or the hole never closed up. During the 1950's and 1960's, she received the diagnosis, very popular in those days, you have a heart murmur.

She was also experiencing fainting spells due to a condition called Atrial Fibrillation (afib), which gave her a few experiences with the 'paddles', since chemical attempts were not successful at bringing her back in rhythm. Then twelve years ago, she underwent the open heart surgery, ASD repair. Fortunately, the flap of skin was still there, so no need for grafting of skin and the hole was closed up. She came through that successfully, recovered fairly quickly, began walking around our neighborhood and was back at work as a dental hygienist three months later; I called her my hero. During her job as a dental hygienist, Kathi served in another vocation for her patients, as she listened to their life stories, became part of their families, ultimately through three generations and was their personal counselor.

Kathi accompanied me to every class of 'our' five year formation in the diaconate program; culminating in my ordination on June 7, 2014. Your life is rolling along. The kids are doing well; the grandkids are growing before your very eyes (and being added to). You and your spouse are making travel plans for that two week trip to Hawaii and your consulting business is clicking, in fact you have to turn away work. Over the years, your spouse's health is suffering more and more.

Nine years ago, Kathi was diagnosed with a disease you and not many other people have heard of; Mycobacterium avium Complex Infection or in the vernacular:MAC/I . In fact, when she was first diagnosed, our county health district office wanted to quarantine our home, because they thought she had tuberculosis.

Pulmonary Mycobacterium avium complex (MAC) infection is a type of non-tuberculous mycobacterial (NTM) infection. It is relatively common and continues to pose significant therapeutic challenges. In addition, in many instances the role of MAC in pulmonary pathology remains controversial[6]. Several different syndromes are caused by Mycobacterium avium complex (MAC). Disseminated infections are usually associated with HIV infection. Less commonly, pulmonary disease in nonimmunocompromised persons is a result of infection with MAC.[7]

Again, I am sharing from my perspective, the maladies which continue to train me as a caregiver.

MAC is 'treated/controlled' via a three antibiotic chemo cocktail taken daily for 18 months. The side effects of this cocktail are devastating to the patient and they were devastating to my wife. When she first started in June 2006, she lasted three months on the regimen and quit because it takes the life out of you. Her patients and doctors alike, told her she looked 'lifeless'. However, she restarted the regimen, knowing the alternative was not acceptable.

Mycobacteriumavium complex (MAC) is intrinsically resistant to many antibiotics and antituberculosis drugs but is fairly susceptible to the following agents:

- *Macrolides (eg, clarithromycin, azithromycin)*
- *Rifamycins (eg, rifampin, rifabutin)*
- *Ethambutol*
- *Clofazimine*
- *Fluoroquinolones (eg, ciprofloxacin, levofloxacin, moxifloxacin)*
- *Aminoglycosides (eg, amikacin, streptomycin)*

In general, MAC infection is treated with 2 or 3 antimicrobials for at least 12 months. Commonly used first-line drugs include macrolides (clarithromycin or azithromycin), ethambutol, and rifamycins (rifampin, rifabutin). Aminoglycosides, such as streptomycin and amikacin, are also used as additional agents.

Aerosolized amikacin has been found to be an effective adjunctive therapy in a small case series.[8]

In Kathi's case, she was treated with azithromycin, ethambutol and rifabutin orally for 18 months in her first bout. In her second bout, she was referred to country's specialist on MAC at University of Texas Health Science Center Northeast (UTHSCNE) in Tyler, Texas, which is a 6 and ½ hour one way drive, even with the higher speed limit toll roads in between San Antonio and Tyler. Because of the effects of the cocktail, her local infectious disease doctor prescribed the doses to be taken three days a week, instead of the daily doses she experienced the first round. Additionally, the specialist in Tyler augmented her treatment with daily dose of amikacin, which was administered through a nebulizer we have at home. The second bout of MAC was 'eradicated' after one year of the cocktail. For MAC, this does not mean 'remission'. Just means it is dormant. Since Kathi has had two bouts, this means she will probably be administered a lifelong regimen.

After her first visit to Tyler, with subsequent chest x-ray and CT scan, we became aware of something called bronchiectasis. Apparently, she had an advanced stage for her age.

Bronchiectasis is a condition in which the lungs' airways are abnormally stretched and widened. This stretching and widening is caused by mucus blockage. More and more mucus builds up in the airways, allowing bacteria to grow. This leads to infection.

Bronchiectasis can develop at any age. It begins most often in childhood, but symptoms may not appear until much later. Bronchiectasis can occur as part of a birth defect or as a result of injury or other diseases, like tuberculosis, pneumonia and influenza.

- *Symptoms include:*
- *Coughing (worse when lying down)*
- *Shortness of breath*
- *Abnormal chest sounds*

- *Daily production of large amounts of coughed up mucus*
- *Chest pain*
- *Clubbing (flesh under your fingernails and toenails becomes thicker)*

Bronchiectasis cannot be cured. But with proper treatment most people with bronchiectasis can live a normal life.[9]

Treatments include:

- *Antibiotics for infection*
- *Bronchodilator medicines to open airways*
- *Mucus-thinning medicines*
- *Expectorants to help you cough up mucus*
- *Physical therapy techniques to help clear mucus*
- *Oxygen therapy (if the disease is widespread)*
- *Surgery (if the disease is in only one part of the lung or if there is a lot of bleeding)*

The specialist in Tyler also prescribed an aerosol saline to assist in the control regimen for the bronchiectasis. So Kathi spent 90 minutes a day, 45 minutes upon awaking and 45 minutes before going to sleep, administering the aerosol medicines. On our last visit to Tyler, I posed the question regarding bronchiectasis. The doctor told Kathi, that it would not necessarily shorten her life, but would definitely have an impact on her quality of life.

Kathi also contracted an infection in her lungs called pseudomonas and apparently this 'dropped' down from her sinuses. She had to have the sinus infection surgically removed four years earlier.

A pseudomonas infection is caused by a very common type of bacteria called Pseudomonas aeruginosa (say "soo-duh-MOH-nuss ay-roo-jee-NOH-suh").

Healthy people often carry these bacteria around without knowing it and without having any problems. Sometimes these germs cause minor problems like swimmer's ear and hot tub rash. But for people who are weak or ill, these germs can cause very serious—even deadly— infections in any part of the body. [10]

I apologize for all the technical information, but as a caregiver and a service to you, I felt compelled to share what you as a caregiver must begin to realize. You must become 'smart' in the care of your loved one, so that you may become an effective advocate for your loved one. The hardest part for me is learning to correctly say the medicine names and which illness they were supposed to combat. I also had (have) trouble keeping the counter acting drugs aligned (in my head).

I have added a few pages with medical acronyms and a Glossary of Terms. These are by no means an all-inclusive list; but they are ones that have 'popped' up during my wife's care.

Over the past three years, her atrial fibrillation has become one nagging thing that will not go away; plus 'they' noted a leaking mitral valve in her heart on an echocardiogram in June 2011.

Toward the end of 2012, Kathi was tiring of her afib and began investigating a procedure called ablation. She asked her cardiologist at the time and he referred her to a specialist within the field of cardiology, called an electrophysiologist.

When the heart beats with a normal rhythm, electricity flows from the top of the heart to the bottom of the heart, causing the heart muscle to contract and moving the blood through the body. In AFib, the electricity flows chaotically and the bottom chambers of the heart contract irregularly.[11]

In certain instances, medications or cardioversion may not control your atrial fibrillation effectively. A specially trained cardiologist (called an electrophysiologist) may perform a surgical procedure called an ablation to fix your atrial fibrillation. A radiofrequency ablation is done through a catheter threaded into your heart to send low-voltage, high-frequency electricity into the area of your heart that is causing the irregular electrical rhythm. This destroys the small amount of tissue causing the abnormal heart beat and may totally cure the AFib. [12]

In some cases, surgery on your heart may be needed to treat your AFib. The Maze procedure is a type of surgery where small cuts are placed in the upper chamber of the heart (atria) to help the conduction of electricity to be regular. This procedure may also be done through small incisions or catheters threaded into the heart. [13]

Kathi received her first ablation, basically a process which feeds a camera through one thigh artery and the 'tool' through the other, on

December 5, 2013. The effects were successful for approximately two weeks and Kathi underwent several cardioversions (the shock paddles), before undergoing her second ablation on April 29, 2014. The doctor came out to the waiting room and told me he had done an 'extensive' ablation. I had no idea what that meant, but it did not 'fix' the ablation and at a follow-up appointment two weeks later, I told the doctor the effect it did have on Kathi; you took the life out of her. And Kathi got to experience several more cardioversions, to no avail.

Diagnosis

The premise for this book begins with the next few entries.

September 22, 2014.

We arrive at PCP's office for appointment; what a blessing! He is very thorough and comprehensive; he is even ordering echocardiogram through Kathi's cardiologist, and a bunch of labs, including a couple of tests for Amyloidosis, the disease that took Kathi's father. We got here at 2:40 P.M., per staff's telephone call on September 18 at 6:00 P.M. Trouble is we check in and the assistant tells us we're on the notes but not the calendar, so at least we get to wait. He told her she looks anemic and wants her to come back in 2-3 weeks. He told her to go back on metroprolol; 25 mg, 25 mg, 2 X/day. I felt relieved somewhat, we came out of that office with a plan of action, however it was too late in the day to go to the lab, which was closed, so we have to come back tomorrow morning.

September 23, 2014.

We arrive at the lab at 9:00 and Kathi gave her blood, not without difficulty as her low blood pressure presents a challenge to the attendants, but could not produce urine, so they gave her a sample bottle to bring back when she could later today. Plus, I had appointment at my ENT to open up my right ear. So I took Kathi home, got her settled in and went to my doctor's appointment. Man, did that hurt! But, at least now I do not have that plugged up feeling/sense in the back of my head and I can hear much better.

I sit with Kathi all day, she slept, but every once in a while, I would wake her up and prod her to try and produce urine for the sample bottle. No such luck. At 4:20 P.M., the lab calls and wants to know if we're going to bring sample today, they have to know by 4:30, I told them I would call them at 4:30, which I did and asked if we could bring it first thing in the morning, they said yes.

Kathi's BFF came over in the late afternoon and began preparing a week's worth of meals for us. At 4:45 P.M. Kathi wakes up, still cannot produce (urine), but is hungry, gets up and goes into the living room to watch the evening news. After eating, at 5:18, she says she is not feeling that good and is going back to bed. At 5:20 PM I go in to check on her and she tells me she cannot catch her breath, does her emergency inhaler and wants to go to ER. I hand her a pair of lounge pants to put on and she tells me to call EMS, she still couldn't catch her breath, which I immediately did as she began pulling on the pants.

I go and tell Kathi's BFF, she asks what can she do and I tell her to just continue what you're doing.

EMS got to the house within 10 minutes. They came in and asked about Kathi's health history, while another EMT got her sitting on the living room couch and they took her BP (we could not get reading on home machine); which was 42/27 and she was still awake. They immediately got her strapped down on stretcher and said they were still going to do some work in the truck like an EKG and I could follow them to the ER. About 25 minutes later, the driver came out and told me they would be driving without the lights/sirens (I found this odd) and for me not to drive crazy and follow them. They left in front of the house about 15 minutes later. I lost them in the parking lot at the hospital and parked my truck and went into the ER entrance and they called me a few minutes later to fill out paperwork and then a few minutes after that, they told me I could go in with her in room 12. Met her attending nurse, and while she was still more or less getting Kathi settled and specialists were coming and going and doing portable x-ray, lab draws, the ER attending physician came in and noticed 'something' on the telemetry read-outs and call was made to move Kathi to room 8 (across from 'nurses' station). As they were prepping Kathi for the move; something else occurred and everything went into fast forward mode; running her down the hallway to the new room. They got her into the new room, put up a partition/screen separating the view of Kathi from the floor. I was kind of sitting on counter and I could see the telemetry monitor from my position. 'Help' started coming out of the woodwork, there are now a dozen people in this room, torn packages and paper is being thrown all over the place as these professional caregivers are fighting to save my wife's life. The telemetry monitoring Kathi's pulse flat lined and her HR went to zero, I saw an attendant grab the 'paddles' and an eternity later, the attending physician hollered "I got a pulse, I got a pulse!". This is something I never want to witness again.

Her white blood cells are high, she has an infection? Her kidneys are not functioning, that is why she could not go to the bathroom. They're asking me if she has been complaining about belly pain, because it is significantly distended. I tell them no, she only complains about the arthritis in her hips in that region. They 'suspect' an infected gall bladder. Hallelujah, they did an echocardiogram. After getting Kathi 'stabilized' (and I use the term loosely), they began peeling back the onion, as it continued until 4:00 AM, they find a 6mm bacterial/vegetative growth on the mitral valve in her heart – this showed up on the echocardiogram. This growth is a definitive sign of an infection; something called endocarditis, however they must now begin taking lab samples and culture for three different types of 'bugs'.

Endocarditis is an infection of the inner lining of your heart (endocardium). Endocarditis generally occurs when bacteria or other germs from another part of your body, such as your mouth, spread through your bloodstream and attach to damaged areas in your heart. Left untreated, endocarditis can damage or destroy your heart valves and can lead to life-threatening complications. Treatments for endocarditis include antibiotics and, in certain cases, surgery.

Endocarditis is uncommon in people with healthy hearts. People at greatest risk of endocarditis have damaged heart valves, artificial heart valves or other heart defects.[14]

The three suspect infections are Sepsis, which everyone is praying is not the culprit because of its propensity for moving throughout the body in the bloodstream; and Streptococcus and Staph. For each, the regimen is a 6 week combat with daily doses of antibiotics.

Kathi's BFF brings prepared meals to all the family members in the waiting room. The waiting room was full of family and friends, in this family, those two terms family and friends are synonymous. If you are a friend of a cousin, you become a cousin.

Caregiver

A caregiver comes from all walks of life. My personal biography as I arrived at this opportunity in my life may, or may not, have prepared me for this life event, I cannot say. I will say, that I previously received experience with our daughter twenty years ago and my mother-in-law, five years ago. What I can say is that being a caregiver changes your demeanor, physiology, philosophy and perspective. Up to this point, I had accomplished much in over forty years in the Aerospace Industry. I am used to making split second decisions and taking the steps to implement the solution based on a 'big picture' perspective.

39

My wife's suffering has changed that part of my persona and humbled me. I'm not saying I was necessarily an arrogant or hard-charging individual, but it has brought me down a peg or two. It has brought me to my knees. I have no clue what the big picture is, to the extent that it has paralyzed me. Throughout my career, I have talked in a negative way about folks who could not make a decision, hampered by analysis paralysis. Yet here I am, suffering the same malady. I do not have access to the resources or the training to be an effective cog in this medical gear. I and my wife are at the mercy of the medical industry with all its pros and cons, just as with any human organization. Now, I try and have been somewhat successful, after the fact, in making 'suggestions' to the staff to review or consider something in the diagnosis/prognosis for Kathi's care. This of course, is based on my personal knowledge of my wife's medical history, which I have experienced with her and my experience as a 'mechanic'.

As a Catholic Christian and deacon in the Church, my faith sustains me and I pray, that I am a rock for my wife and family. I also pray with and without words for Kathi's well-being and healing—to remove the suffering from her, calm her anxiety and fears, and give her peace. Selfishly, I carefully word my prayers, knowing that God's will is not necessarily my own and knowing that our prayers are answered, however not exactly the way we have in mind and heart and not in the timeframe we wish. I have come across this phenomenon on numerous occasions as part of the human condition, when praying to our Creator.

In one long-term acute care facility (LTAC), a chaplain (I assumed he was Catholic) came by to offer prayer and at the time Kathi was no longer NPO, so I asked if he brought Holy Communion and he said no. Upon learning I was a deacon, he told me, "You're a deacon, you can bring it." This kind of backed me up and made me feel ill will towards him, but then I realized, maybe that was not his calling or ministry. He was right; I can bring Holy Communion and again, it made me realize, perhaps there is a need.

I have learned the most important role for the caregiver is to be present to your loved one and to be her advocate, when it comes to her medical care. The second thing I have learned, and witnessed, is compassion for those in similar suffering scenarios who are without caregivers and advocates. My many walks through the hospital hallways have laid this directly in my path. Who is looking out for them? Here I go again, trying to be all things to all people. It has taken me awhile, but I know I cannot do it all myself. Same with our priests, doctors, educators and those dedicated to the care of others. Over the course of my life, I have for the most part considered others. I guess the current vernacular is 'other-minded'.

4. The Caregiver as a Sufferer

I t only became apparent to me about four months ago, that as a somewhat 'healthy' person and this is indicative of my naiveté or limited perspective; thinking only sick people suffer. I realized and it came as an epiphany to me; that my suffering has occurred as a result of my caring for my ill wife, daughter, mother-in-law and father-in-law over the last 20 years, remembering my own father's losing battle with diabetes and heart disease 32 years ago and my mother's four year bout and demise with cancer 45 years ago. Of those remaining, my daughter still struggles along physically crippled and blind from medicinal (prednisone) side effects due to her Lupus. And it is not because I stuck my head in the sand, when trials and tribulations raised their ugly head in our family. Perhaps my general demeanor and disposition lend themselves as a calming (or maddening) influence on those around me.

What is known is there are nurses who care for you when you are in the hospital, but they are not watching over you every minute. They too are human and even if they were not, machines break down as well.

They are not at your home caring for the sick and invalid spouse, sibling, child, unless you have home health care and again they are typically not there 24/7.

What is not known, is that it is you who helps your wife, daughter, mother-in-law out of bed at night to help them to the bathroom or bring them a drink of water in the middle of the night, pick them up off the floor because they have fallen; or clean up their sheets, bathe them or feed them because they are not able. You begin to 'childproof' your home, putting in nightlights, so they can see in the middle of the night. Their frailty begins to affect your sleep habits as well, having to be alert when they try to be independent and tend to themselves.

My career has trained me for this, putting in 10-16 hour days or until they 'kick' me out, sitting by my wife's bedside, whether she is asleep or awake. I put in a 28 hour day on a project as recent as March 2, 2014; thinking even then when I had finished, I should have this much devotion to my ministries. Holding her hand amidst all the wires, cables and tubes, being careful not to yank on any them by mistake, but being the calming influence as best I can, still being wholly unable to truly empathize with my wife's condition and what she is truly feeling. We cannot even imagine, if we have not been there ourselves, you only know that you never want to be in that condition. You pray that this condition be removed from her with all your being.

What my career did not train me for, is patience and stillness. I am unable to 'do' anything and I thrive on being gainfully employed. When your daughter spends a year in hospital care and your wife spends six months pretty much flat on her back in your house before she enters long-term hospital care, a person with my disposition becomes infuriated and frustrated. However, I have been blessed to be able to focus my energies on their care and to become their advocate, since at times, they do not have a voice for themselves. But, I do suffer undo stress as my current contract and project ended and my next one tentatively does not begin until the New Year. This is what happens in the consultant world, when you maintain only one egg in the basket. I am not on Social Security and my 'retirement' is eaten up by health insurance premiums, what's leftover barely covers the monthly grocery bill and we do not eat that much. Thank God, however, that we do have health insurance. I could stand to lose some belly.

5. Prayer

Prayer is the one thing you can definitely provide your loved one. It is the one thing, which you do have control over and since the prayers come from your heart; they are heard. You say you do not know how to pray? What is it that you are wishing for your loved one? Healing, peace, comfort, rest, ease of anxiety, a calming of her fears, focus for yourself, wisdom, understanding, purpose of suffering, doctors make the right decisions or their hands are steady during a procedure, the nurses and staff are caring and compassionate in their care of your loved one? There is a smidgeon of where your prayer can begin, do not forget gratitude/thanksgiving. Take a moment in silence to center your heart in order to hear that little voice in the silence. Sometimes silence is prayer also, in that silent prayer, you may actually hear an answer to your prayer; whether it comes as peace or strengthening of your per-severance to serve your loved one. If you are so distracted (and that is a prayer too, relief) that you seem unable to concentrate and grab a moment of silence in your interior castle, then perhaps you can begin your prayer assault/regimen by praying the Lord's Prayer and from there ask for forgiveness for thinking ill or anger toward your loved one for the little things she is asking for, to the extent you do not get to 'sit down', because you are popping up at her every request/command. After forgiveness, lift up your petition for your loved one, whatever is called for that day, then you always finish with thanksgiving and praise. Prayer also helps you from feeling useless in the care of your loved one.

Heavenly Father,

I come to you seeking your guidance and strength as I watch over my wife Kathi and her care. I know you know what is in my heart before it is formed. This is something I must learn, I do not know what is in my heart, even after it is formed. This is a prayer of thanksgiving for the many blessings, graces and miracles you have gifted this family with, I ask for your continued forbearance and patience. If it be Your will to call her home, I ask you for a hint of understanding of the Mystery of Your Plan. I also ask you to send the Love of Your Son Jesus to surround our grieving family with the Peace of knowing our loved one is safe and home in her heavenly home. We also ask the Blessed Mother Mary to wrap her arms around Kathi as only a mother can provide comfort to her children.

We lift up these prayers through Your Son Jesus, who lives in unity with You and the Holy Spirit, one God, forever and ever. Amen.

The following prayer is from Kathi's aunt who prayed this during the days before Kathi's heart surgery, in response to her anxiety concerning the surgery. Her aunt asks that only the Spirit (Ruach HaKodesh) from which this prayer came, be given the credit.

Messiah, Y'shua, YOU are SAR SHALOM, the Prince of Peace. You said by Your Word, "*Peace I leave with you, My peace I give unto you: not as the world gives, give I unto you. Let not your heart be troubled, neither let it be afraid.*" And again at the mouth of Paul You sent us this truth, "*For Yah has not given us the spirit of fear; but of power, and of love, and of a sound mind.*"

*Now, we know and understand that anxiety is a form of fear. So, Holy One, we speak the power and authority of Your Word over Kathi, Your **Peace** that passes all understanding, and that the spirit of FEAR, and ANXIETY has NO AUTHORITY over her mind, her heart, her being, for YOUR Spirit abides in her and YOUR Spirit is NOT the spirit of FEAR, but of POWER and of LOVE and of a SOUND MIND!! A mind that does not doubt, but rather trusts in YOU and YOUR MIGHT.*

Holy One, You have been with Kathi so MIGHTILY! You have shown Your GREATNESS, Your GOODNESS, and Your POWER throughout this whole matter in Kathi's life. May it be so that Kathi will think on this truth and this fact; may she take every other thought captive and cast it down to the pulling down of any stronghold of fear...may it be so that whatsoever is TRUE, HONEST, JUST, PURE, LOVELY, OF A GOOD REPORT, WHERE THERE IS VIRTUE, AND WHERE THERE

IS PRAISE...that Kathi will think only on THESE things. We ask this in the Glorious and Powerful Name of our Messiah, Y'shua. For there is NO other Name under Heaven whereby we are saved!!! GLORY To YOU, AWESOME, YAH!!! Ah-mein, and Ah-MEIN!!!

Todah rabah, Abba....Thank You, very much, Abba.

Heavenly Father,

We lift Kathi up to your Healing Presence. We ask for the guidance of your Holy Spirit and that your hands become the surgeons hands as they operate on Kathi tomorrow. Through Your Love, we seek a successful surgery and rapid recovery for Kathi as we will witness the miracle of Your Love. Send the Love of Your Son Jesus to fill the operating room with safety, protection and attention. We ask the Blessed Mother to wrap her arms around Kathi and comfort her as only a mother can. We ask that You ease Kathi's anxiety, calm her fears and let her know Your Peace. Not our Will, Lord, but Yours be done.

For these blessings, we humbly pray through Your Son, Who lives in unity with You and the Holy Spirit, one God, forever and ever. Amen!

6. Advocate

W hen the patient is in the hands of professionals; the role of the caregiver changes to one of advocacy for the patient. You must be vigilant in knowing what her meds are and forever ask questions about what they are doing and giving her. You will become like a bothersome gnat or mosquito to ensure your loved one is being properly cared for and it is your right.

Trust

I'm going to make a general statement at the beginning of this section. For those reading these pages because you are looking for guidance in caring for your loved one, it is probably because you have had minimal healthcare training. That being said, it is best to rely on the experts, who have had the schooling and practical experience in dealing with the illnesses or injuries currently affecting your loved one. This does not mean following sheepishly. If you have a question about your loved one's professional care – ask it, whether it is directly to the doctor, the nurse, staff, facility admin/business office or your health insurance. If they answer in medical lingo and you do not understand it still, ask them to translate so that you can understand. It is important that you are comfortable, without having to stress about that one more thing.

Relationships

As a caregiver, as with anything else, it is important to maintain a congenial relationship(s) with those professionals charged with your loved one's healthcare. You do not necessarily have to learn about their family, their cousin's kids or sister's pets or you may, but the important thing to remember is they are human, like you. Getting mad, screaming and hollering may make you feel 'better?', but when you are finished, your loved one is still flat on her back in a hospital bed and you may have put off the very person who can help your loved one. Talk to them if something is awry, ask a leading question, like; "Is this tube supposed to be full of blood?", "Why is her respirator not on?".

In any relationship, you will be treated as you treat others. In your position as caregiver, you must keep an even demeanor and disposition if you expect the same in return and you will get more accomplished regarding the professional healthcare of your loved one. The professional caregivers will consult with you and discuss your loved one's care with you; you will notice the concern in their eyes and sometimes their own feeling of helplessness or exasperation. Again, calling names or their training into question will not resolve any issue and may ultimately exacerbate the outcome. When you go home or to the gym, you can take it out on the punching bag or the pedals of the bicycle.

Questions

You must learn to ask questions of the care providers:

1. What are you doing?

2. What are you giving her?

3. Why are you doing that?

4. Why are you giving her that medicine, she has not had that before?

5. Why are you checking her sugar? She is not diabetic?

6. Why don't you change this suction tube? It's full of blood.

7. Why don't you change the trach? Someone was thinking about it, because here is a trach replacement kit.

8. Did you have to do that? Couldn't you be a little more gentler? She was asleep.

9. She pooped the bed, do you think it might be time to change the sheets and clean her up?

10. What doctors have been by today? What did they say?

11. What is the plan? Why?

You must also be cognizant of the medicines your spouse, loved one is taking. You must be aware of any side effects of those medicines, and any contradictory interfaces or side effects of all. My wife is taking 14 different medicines, sometimes 18 when she is fighting a bout of MAC. There are certain anti-arrhythmia medicines which do not perform when taken in combination with the anti-biotic(s) regimen required for control/eradication of MAC. You must learn all these variances and constantly observe your loved one's care.

Appendage(s)

Your cell phone becomes an appendage, even carrying it to the bathroom, which the author despised long ago as a manager and learned to leave the cell phone on the desk when using the facilities. You also sleep with your phone at all times, with sound on, whatever your ringtone is, so that you can awake at the first chirp. Mine happens to be the revving of a motorcycle engine.

Be sure not to get a ticket for talking on your cell while driving, know what the local laws say about that. Here in San Antonio, they passed a law prohibiting use of a cell phone while driving, unless you have a hands-free capability. Each major car maker provides this as an option, in addition to some of the wireless phone providers. I'm not saying I invented the internet, but I did have a wireless phone provider install a hands free package in my pickup truck in the parking lot of my facility in 1999, while I was working. Your computer/laptop is maintained close by as well, in its use as a news service broadcast medium.

It was my experience, that it is not so convenient to text patient information on your cell phone, it's much easier (for me) to create the distribution list and email it from my laptop. Call me old fashioned. Be sure that whatever facility you find yourself in, get the Wi-Fi key, password, so you can maintain that communication medium. For me, as consultant who writes for a living, it has been a necessity.

The Call

Looming in the background is the anticipation of receiving the 'phone call' notification. Sometimes, as in my wife's case, I received, not necessarily, the call, but an after the fact update or status notification that an event had occurred and they were able to bring her back around, twice so far as of this writing. And for us, it never seemed to occur during the daylight hours. But, that ominous premonition does not go away and at times makes you go awry, as you combat an attack on your senses and sensibilities from all corners.

7. Rollercoaster

July 7, 2014.

Kathi is not improving; her lungs are fighting with her heart for the same oxygen. She gets wore out from the simplest exertion, such as taking a shower and then she has to take a nap. She sleeps all day and of course at night too. Much like our daughter has done over the last five years. It is having an impact on me when I am at home. On vacation as well, watching her and being drawn into the lack or drain of energy. The upside is, on the 4th of July, she did say she was bored!

I officially started my assignment as Deacon at St. Monica on July 1st in earnest. That evening, I interviewed the parents of seven unrelated children who were being presented for Baptism. The next two days, (not full days) I began setting up my office at the pastoral center. Of course, nothing happens overnight and there were the usual hiccoughs. The laptop does not have current software, cannot be upgraded and the computer guy is in Washington DC for the next week, but it sounds like I will be getting a PC for the rectory office.

This past Saturday July 5, I got to participate in the Baptism of the seven children. It was an amazing and humbling experience. Parents were asking me to bless the symbols they brought and for me to be in the pictures with their children. Our vicar priest was very gracious in allowing me to participate, I am blessed. Yesterday, I served at the 9:00 A.M., 11:00 A.M. and 5:30 P.M. Masses, it has been a month since I served during Pentecost. I was a little rusty at first, proclaimed the Gospel and preached (on the peace and freedom of Jesus), set up and cleared the Altar. My homily seemed to be received very well including by my most ardent critic, Kathi who attended the 11:00 A.M. Mass. I may have said things not well received, but those who may have been offended did not tell me.

One thing to note of interest, being this is my journal and I have posted this previously. As I drew closer to ordination, I was anxious about my 'dying to my old self'. Since ordination, a noticeable change in my thoughts and feelings regarding this has occurred overnight. Whereas, before, my thoughts for the most part were consumed with work and strategies for approaching the next project or what I had done that day and where it should lead in the coming weeks of the project.

Today, a month after ordination, I do not even think about work any longer; not even where the next project is coming from, I'm at peace which is inexpressible except for the groanings of my heart and soul (Romans). My thoughts are focused on my new vocation, along with those which are constantly worried about Kathi's health. She did go to Church yesterday, but went right to bed after our traditional breakfast at Jim's. Today, she is at IHOP with her aunts for sisters' breakfast and already told me this morning, she is thinking about her bed and nap to come.

While reading Nicomachean Ethics by Aristotle, I am faced again with the definition of happiness. I am going to try to describe it in my words.

For me, and that is why Aristotle considered it subjective; it begins with being alive as a sentient being. More than that, however, I have an innate sense of gratitude for being alive. Simply put, I am happy to be here. If I had not been born, I would not have experienced any of this (my arms are wide open) in a void, vacuum, nothingness. As such, my approach to what life brings also differs from many, I accept what comes my way. Emotions do not rule the day, unless the event was self-imposed; then I give myself a good lecture: "What did you expect"?

July 18, 2014.

I'm a little reflective this morning, as I'm fixing to take the girls to the beach and I began thinking about my self-imposed mission to do my part to clean up 'my' beach. This led me to think about our disposable society and culture, which infuses itself all the way to the sanctity and gift of human lives. This phenomenon is not limited to the western culture, but is also eastern, and Saharan. In creation, we are (and should be) stewards to maintain this gift! Yet it appears we are only a cancerous cell in a larger organism. We seem bent on destroying this gift, one way or the other. I'm depressed.

July 25, 2014.

We met with the PCP's Physician Assistant (PA). Kathi is not feeling well, very weak and sleeping all the time. No lab work.

July 28, 2014.

Kathi has a follow-up visit with Infectious Disease (ID) doctor. Her office took the preliminary vitals as office visit protocol and the ID doctor immediately wanted Kathi to go across the parking lot (single lane street wide) to the NE Baptist ER, because of Kathi's low BP 78/44. But, instead, she called Kathi's eletrophysiologist's office, who wanted to know if we could make it to their office across town. I found this kind of odd, but like a sheep, instead of demanding EMS, drove Kathi to their office and saw his partner; who ran an EKG and admitted her to the NW 'Cardiac Short-Stay' hospital for four days. They released her four days later which they seemed to be in a rush to do, but were unable to release her due to Kathis low BP and pulse/ox (could not reach 90). The attendant cardiologist in the hospital was trying to determine why she was fainting/blacking out (hindsight – could it be low BP?). So, I mentioned her arachnoid cyst, maybe it had grown, putting pressure where none was, they did a head CT, an in-house neurologist reviewed it. Discharge instructions said to do 3 follow-up visits; with her PCP, her eletrophysiologist (in 2 weeks) and a neurologist. They relied on my non-medical diagnosis. They did not do an echocardiogram (being a 'cardiac' short stay hospital, just in case; this is sarcasm) or even lab work to determine if she had an infection.

Between this hospital visit and the next on September 23, 2014 (roughly 6 weeks); Kathi was left in limbo by the healthcare industry, while her condition continued to deteriorate and worsen.

August 6, 2014.

This morning while praying the office, the date crossed my mind and heart, echoing through the halls of my memory like it never had before; since my mother's passing on this date in 1965. The tears came gushing out, more so than when the event actually occurred; course I have written in here or elsewhere, that by the time she died, I was cried out. Like a friend told me on the day of my ordination, I have the gift of tears and I told her yes, I have read that in St. John of the Cross' Dark Night of the Soul and St. Teresa de Avila's Interior Castle.

August 7, 2014.

Last night or earlier this morning while awake; God came to me calling me 'Deacon'. I answered, Yes? Father, I am here. He said 'Feed my sheep'. I have no expression or words for the journey I took in probably picoseconds; but touching millennia (eternity) and back. Then I asked "Where have you been?", since I've seemingly experienced a long period of aridity in the desert of my soul. Of course, the realization came that I was the one who had been elsewhere. And then I transitioned to my mom again, thinking about how she spent the last two months of her life in a hospital bed in our living room – which was an epiphany as I fast forwarded to four years ago, as Kathi's mom was dying in a hospital bed in the living room of her house. A bed my mother-in-law asked me to move from her bedroom to the front room, not an easy task, disassembling it and reassembling it, without instructions or assistance. These two hospital beds seemed to provide a framework of sorts or bookends to my formation. Then I thought about my wife and my daughter, which made me think of myself as a witness to suffering. This then led me to realize I am suffering as witnessing the suffering of my loved ones. All this time, I have thought, written or said; I am unable to empathize with those suffering, because I have not suffered. God opened the window and released my soul to feed His sheep! Oh what a glorious blessing, I have been set free; my stoicism has been a crutch and holding me back. I can still be the rock of the family.

8. Keystone Cops

Perhaps the title of this section is wanting, but then so were we. Maybe a better title would be Abeyance, because that is exactly how we felt all summer, particularly the last six weeks before Kathi's most recent hospitalization, which coincidentally, began with a hospital stay.

August 14 – September 22, 2014.

We are attempting to get serious about Kathi's care and determine why she continues to pass out, black out, fall and lose her balance; as all the specialists (you name them) have no clue and scratch their collective heads.

August 14 2014.

I conferenced in with my insurance provider's Medical Policy and Referral Intake Specialist to determine issues with processing of Kathi's various referrals and why they are not approved in a timely manner. Why an out of network pulmonologist is approved, yet any processes (CT Scan, lab work, X-rays, medicines; his basic tools) he orders are disapproved after we have already made the one-way six and ½ hour drive. Thank goodness, the specialist is in Tyler and not someplace like New Hampshire, Seattle or Milwaukee. Kathi is consistently being turned away from established appointments with local in-network specialists, as well. The specialist offices are attempting to pull the referrals in, but to no avail AND no one is calling Kathi to let her know one way or another and she is in no condition to 'fight' this battle. And they do not release any information to me, because she is an adult and it is a 'privacy' issue for her husband of 42 years. This is premise for a whole other tome.

My insurance provider shows annual referrals for 2014 for Kathi's in-network ID Dr. and the out of network leading MAC specialist in Tyler. However, there are no referral requests for lung CT Scans from either doctor (I told my insurance provider, because they were disapproved)– and part of the reason for my call is to find out why the referrals were disapproved. Their response was they had not received any, digging in to find who and why the lying.

August 15, 2014.

I called Kathi's PCP's office to determine status of referral for Kathi's in-network local pulmonologist. I left a voice mail (LVM).

August 18, 2014.

It has been a great weekend! Friday at the Assumption Mass (bi-lingual), I said some of the intercessory/prayers of the faithful in Spanish. On Saturday, I took Kathi, yes Kathi, to one of our granddaughter's birthday party! And the day before, Kathi made me take her to Target to get some presents. Then yesterday, she joined me at the 5:30 PM Mass and then we went out to eat dinner. Halleluah! God is Good! All the time!

August 19, 2014.

I called the PCP's office to determine status of referrals for pulmonologist and neurologist-follow-up requirement from hospital discharge on Aug 3.

August 21, 2014.

I called the electrophysiologist's office and he was still in procedures. We are awaiting his decision and follow-up appointment.

August 22, 2014.

All my joy from last week-end has been tempered by yesterday's events. Kathi has been saying her heart rate has been elevated, but does not feel like she is in afib. She went to regularly scheduled appointment with her infectious disease doctor, who in turn wanted to put her directly in the hospital next door. Her heart rate was elevated and her blood pressure was 76/44. Kathi's entire body language coming out of the doctor's office was not one I want to see again – a complete resignation and loss of hope.

From there, we drove to her eletrophysiologist office for an EKG and a decision. The EKG took five minutes and then we were told doctor was in procedures and would review the EKG when he was done – and that we should go and wait for their call. It was around lunchtime so we went and had some delicious Greek food. Silly me, I wanted to go back to the waiting room. Kathi prevailed wanting to go home, pack a hospital bag, change clothes and take a nap. We finally got call at 7:00 PM, telling us to come back at 9:30 A.M.

August 23, 2014.

Visiting with Kathi's electrophysiologist was not a pleasant experience; the man had come to the end of his expertise, rubbing his hands through what little hair he had left (I should talk). He was not full of good news. For starters, I asked him, "What was the next step?". Kathi asked him: "What are my options?". We talked about a pacemaker, which we knew was not an option, but we let the doctor verify the answer. A pacemaker basically ignores high heart rates. Then there was a discussion of surgical intervention and when I reminded him that Kathi had pericarditis when she was 19, which was not a good option because of the inherent scar tissue from that event, her ASD repair twelve years ago, as well as her current range of scar tissue occurrences. During these conversations, the Doctor was placing phone calls to partners and colleagues, who validated the responses or negated the options, if you will, while rubbing his hands through his imaginary hair. Finally, the doctor said there was 'possibly' one more option – yet another ablation from a recognized regional specialist in Austin. This specialist is one who feels he can get it done, no matter the challenge. Turns out that one of our diaconate classmates had the procedure performed by this doctor. In any case, we receive the contact information for this specialist in Austin, who is, yep you guessed it, out of network, however this did not deter us. Meanwhile, Kathi's heart is still in afib. We went home.

August 25, 2014.

I spoke to a staff member at the PCP's office, she found Kathi's info, but placed me on hold. I was transferred to another staff member who informed me that referral process was 'stymied', because insurance denied it due to incorrect policy number. Once I gave her the correct Insurance provider policy number; the referrals were approved that day!

August 26, 2014.

I talked to the PCP staff again and the blanket referrals for both the pulmonologist and neurologist had been approved through February 2015, as soon as she gave Insurance provider the right policy number – again we had to initiate the follow-up to find out the staff had made an error. Someone will die with this kind of efficiency and compassion. But, more importantly, you must be your own advocate and vigilant about your healthcare.

I called the electrophysiologist's office in Austin for appointment; of course he is out of network, we have been going down the wrong rabbit hole for 2 years and he was fixing to send us even further. Anyway, appointment is set for November 11 at 11:30.

I called Insurance provider about another eletrophysiologist who is in network, because I do not feel Kathi will be able to make the one hour drive. They mentioned another who happens to be in her local electrophysiologist's group.

I talked to Insurance provider and she said the referrals in the system are valid for pulmonologist and neurologist. I suppose I'm gun shy.

I called and Kathi has an appointment with pulmonologist on Sept 2 at 9:00 A.M.

I left voice mail with staff at PCP's office at 2:05 PM, she returned my call at 3:15, which I missed. I left message with staff at neurologist's office. She returned my call at 6:15 PM, which I missed.

August 27, 2014.

I spoke to staff at neurologist's office. Kathi has an appointment at 4:20 PM on Sept 3, and we are to fill out various new patient forms from website before arriving.

September 2, 2014.

Upon seeing her, the pulmonologist told Kathi, you do not look good. Of course she doesn't, that's why she is here. A vibrant young woman coming to your office using a walker and gasping for breath, and his diagnosis was no better. He told her that her MAC had come back, yet again, just by the symptoms Kathi was relating to him. The pulmonologist requested lung CT scan and discussed perhaps referral to another local electrophysiologist who trained under the Austin specialist, in lieu of driving to Austin. I told the pulmonologist that Kathi would not make the hour trip to Austin and I told him we would be cancelling her appointment with the out of network ID doctor, later this month in Tyler. The electrophysiologist was first doctor Kathi visited relative to undergoing ablation procedure, referred by her then cardiologist. She felt he was too young and asked him how many times he had performed this procedure, he replied a dozen. Kathi then went to the one who actually performed the two ablation procedures on December 5, 2013 and April 29, 2014. She felt more comfortable with him and his experience. Hindsight is 20/20.

September 3, 2014.

We met with the neurologist and he told Kathi, that her passing out, fainting and blacking out/losing balance was not due to her arachnoid cyst, but he did refer her to an internal ENT.

September 10, 2014.

I took Kathi to spinal clinic appointment, referred by the PCP, but referral not received? No, after being turned away, I got home and called the insurance provider who informed that blanket referral expired on August 25, 2014.

I called Insurance provider about Spinal clinic blanket referral expiration and pulmonologist's CT scan referral. I was told the CT scan was approved for August 14 through September 13. I called pulmonologist's office to make appointment for CT scan, got it for Friday September 12.

September 12, 2014.

I had breakfast with one of my grand-daughters at her elementary school for grandparent's day. She was very happy to see me and we got to talk and visit, but she did tell me the new school year was not going too good. It is so sad to see such a young child so stressed.

Kathi's aunt took her to her CT scan. Kathi has been prohibited from driving since her last hospital visit last week-end of July, pending doctors' determination and resolution of Kathi's passing out episodes.

Then later in the day, one of our other grand-daughters broke her left arm/separated from her shoulder at school, she went to one hospital ER and was ambulanced to another which had better pediatric surgery. The next two days felt like two weeks. And tonight, we had an awesome thunderstorm which put the lights out in the hospital for a little while, until the back-up generators kicked in. I still had to walk down the stairs, because the elevators were still out, our grand-daughter's room was only on the third floor, I survived.

September 13, 2014.

Fortunately, it was going to be laparoscopic surgery, two rods through her arm bones to connect to her shoulder. She only spent one night in the hospital. I told people at church I felt like Job. I knew that was wrong as soon as it came out.

September 15, 2014.

Today, I thought I was losing Kathi and the New Testament reading, 1 COR 13:13[15] for the day is her favorite, again I thought that was an omen too – and once more "O ye of little faith!".

September 17, 2014.

I'm beginning to come to end of my rope. I'm afraid to leave Kathi home alone, yet I have to work, even though I'm 'retired'. I talked to Insurance provider relative to Home Health care. He said we were 100% covered with no limit and that PCP had to initiate referral.

I called the PCP's office at 4:15 PM and LVM with staff to obtain appointment for Kathi with PCP. She returned my call at 5:00, which I missed.

September 18, 2014.

I called PCP's office at 10:00 requesting appointment. I LVM again at 3:00 PM with staff. Staff returned my call at 6:00 PM and our appointment is at 2:45 PM on September 22.

9. Journal

This section is aptly entitled and will follow my personal daily log or journal entries and some may include information contained within email notifications of my wife's status or progress. Approximately two weeks in, our son took over the responsibility of informing family and friends about Kathi's status.

September 24, 2014.

Kathi arrives at the Intensive Care Unit (ICU), room 408 directly across from the nurses' station. She is connected to practically every piece of medical equipment known to man. She is intubated with a breathing tube through her mouth and down her throat, which is connected to a respirator. She also has a Nasogastric (NG) tube through her nose and into her stomach for feeding, which is connected to a bag on a stand. She also has a catheter attached to her urethra for relieving urine when nature calls; this is connected to a bag (more like a plastic box, with a junction tube connected for emptying) and also maintains a constant monitor on her body temperature. And of course, she is connected to a heart monitor at seven places on her body and the obligatory pulse/ox monitor on one of her fingers, earlobes or even forehead. They are constantly taking blood samples for culturing; something called blood gas and complete blood count (CBC) levels. Family members continue to come by, check on her and stay. Kathi received Anointing of the Sick.

September 25, 2014.

As a precautionary measure, they inserted a drain tube into her gall bladder. They have not ruled out that the gall bladder may also be a source of infection, but at the same time, they just want to move this out of the equation as they prepare Kathi for the ultimate heart surgery, which is required due to her 'badly' leaking mitral valve. Family and friends are supporting us today as well, with their presence, their prayers, Scripture readings, devotions and hymns.

10:30 PM. Yesterday's entries were written before we went to the hospital, where we are now. Thank God! Kathi said she wanted to go to the hospital when she did and thank God, she then said to call the EMS and thank God they got to our house and got Kathi to the hospital when they did. She would have died in my truck. Her potassium levels were elevated and that is one of the reasons why her kidneys were not working. Her body was shutting down.

September 26, 2014.

Kathi has been in the hospital basically since Tuesday evening, when she coded in the ER, perhaps in the EMS ride on the way to the hospital as well. I will find out when I get a copy of the run report, a new term I learned while asking a nurse about getting a copy of the turnover log from the EMS to the ER. She kept saying ED; internally, it is referred to as the Emergency Department, more to add to my growing list of medical lingo and terminology. There is a dizzying array of acronyms and slang that are short – I understand it provides for a ready reference relative to the condition of the patient. Kathi's heart monitor continues to reflect a ventricular tachycardia (v-tach) rhythm . I had a conference today with two cardiologists, one from Kathi's electro-physiologists' group and one working for the hospital, an infectious disease doctor working for the hospital and two surgeons on staff. The acute care/lead doctor working for the hospital continues to say her condition is 'guarded'. Good news today, Kathi is breathing in addition to the ventilator doing the job, so that is good and the weaning protocol is working; and is a good indicator she will be taken off the ventilator today. Two cultures have come back verifying the infection in her heart, Endocarditis. They are waiting for final culture and will determine course of direct action via antibiotic regimen, a six week protocol. This condition may eventually require surgical removal and may be accomplished during surgery to replace her mitral valve.

One of Kathi's cousins; a medical sales consultant, God bless him, loving and concerned about his cousin Kathi, annoyed one of the potential surgeons by doing a 'sales' call for a more expedient culturing process, he is currently selling to his clients. The doctor pointed his finger at Kathi's cousin, telling him he was offensive. Not to be deterred, he kept on talking; I had to pull him away. After that, I was a little more vigilant about who would talk to Kathi's doctors and nurses; nobody but me. You will note much later in this ordeal, I had not improved my position as sergeant at arms.

September 27, 2014.

Today is one of our grandson's birthday. I ask the attending cardiologist for the week-end; if he could check the 'system' for any other echocardiograms which may have been accomplished. He comes back about an hour later and tells me the only one he can find for Kathi is dated in June 2011, and there is a note about a leaking mitral valve.

Kathi is a little more awake today, when she is awake, but is sleeping mostly. She will be on ventilator through Monday at least; the doctor began turning down the ventilator/respirator earlier today.

They have eliminated staph as the source of the infection in her heart; that is a good thing. But, now they have had to re-culture to isolate and determine which bug has caused the infection. Whatever the bug, the infectious disease doctor has said it will still require a 4-6 week antibiotic regimen. I am not able to attend Jovan's scheduled birthday party. One of her cousins returning from our grandson's birthday party took a picture of Kathi in all her vulnerability and posted it on facebook. I am beside myself, I asked they immediately remove and that they had no right. They apologized and said they didn't know. I told them I knew that. From that point on, my visiting rules or what not to do took on a bizarre turn as I tried to cover everything imaginable, since it seemed some generations are still learning 'soft skills' or hospital protocol.

September 28, 2014.

I'm continuing to write down questions as I think of them or as they come back to me. This ICU room has a little tablet on the table and that is what I am using to write down and ask questions of the doctors when they come around.

Again, I receive the 'guarded' comment in response to Kathi's condition. I do not know why or what difference it makes now, but I am curious to know what transpired in the EMS truck. Today seems to be the wrong day to ask that question as the admin/business office is closed today and asking the nurse (who's new to this system or maybe that's the standard response, says she just moved here from Austin) generates the deer in the headlight look.

What is endocarditis? Response; it is a bacteria, in your wife's case, is a long-term development and grows on scar tissue. Kathi has internal and external scar tissue on her heart, including congenital and pericardial, as well as from her lungs.

What is the risk factor for administering an echocardiogram? Is it like x-rays, MRIs or CT scans for example?

Why would a heart specialist not order one? Is an electro-physiologist not aware of echocardiogram? Is it not part of their tool box? Yes, they do not generally use it, because by the time a patient arrives to them for service, they assume it has already been accomplished.

Is an echocardiogram a general tool for a cardiologist regardless of specialty/training? Especially for difficult, challenging patients when the symptoms are there? Kathi's PCP called for it/referred it through her cardiologist 5 days ago. There are some common symptoms for a leaky heart valve, endocarditis and MAC. Fatigue, night sweats and anemia.

The acute care/lead Dr. S (pulmonologist by training) dialed down the respirator to 10, increasing Kathi's breathing work, will dial down her sedation early in the morning. That did not last long, they turned up the oxygen levels as she was breathing too shallow.

September 29, 2014.

Dr. S turned the respirator down from 10 to 8 and they began taking her off the sedation at 3:00 A.M.. By 10:00, she was completely off, well at least she was no longer receiving any, I do not know how long it takes for the body to be completely rid of the drugs. He continued to say that Kathi's condition was guarded and that it was too early for a prognosis of any kind.

The infectious disease doctor said they have isolated the infection to streptococcus will treat with penicillin for four weeks, he prefers six, but they will be closely monitoring her condition and strength for the imminent surgery, the sooner the better.

Her PCP visited, says Kathi has a long road to go, the gall bladder is not infected, now we will attack infection and we need to address the leaky valve soonest. Cardiologist verified bug and that we must vigilantly monitor Kathi. One of the surgeon's visited and mentioned the surgery is on the periphery while we fight the infection and Kathi gains strength; the gall bladder tube may eventually work itself out/lose, it is expected, do not be alarmed. Gall bladder right now is not the culprit, but was a pseudo victim of the body shutting down.

I know people these days propose marriage and end relationships on Facebook (FB). I have been hesitant to blast Kathi's information to the cyber nebula population, but as her text message and voicemail grows, maybe I can get this 'out there', so I can save her phone for my daughter, son and grandchildren who want to hear Gaga's voice on Kathi's greeting message.

First of all, I want to say thank you for all the love and prayers coming her way, please, please continue, so that we all and bystanders will witness the power of prayer as we have in the past. "Lord, I believe, help me with my unbelief"[16].

For those of you who may not know or not on the various distribution lists and I'm technically inept at creating blast text messages and need some training, as I am a minimalist and reluctant to repeat anything, I appreciate the ability of technology as an instrument of convenience to assist us in our ever increasingly busy day. But, at the same time, technology removes the intimacy and interface that we humans as a species require. "Born Again, Human" BB King[17]. "Human Touch" The Boss[18].

Kathi was brought to the hospital by EMS (she told me to call) last Wednesday evening about 6:00 PM after being attended to within the ambulance for about 25/30 minutes in front of our house. Without going into details, they brought her 'back' in the ER and she is in ICU. It appears we have finally caught the culprits for Kathi's weakness over these last 6 months. She has an infection in heart called endocarditis, (they just determined the bug streptococcus today through various cultures and re-cultures) and a leaky heart valve. You can GTS both and see that there are common symptoms for both and you'll recognize Kathi's symptoms over the last six months. It wasn't until they did an echo cardiogram (her PCP actually called for it when we were in his office on Tuesday) on Wednesday they discovered the bacterial 6mm growth inside her heart and the leaky valve. As of this morning, and throughout the day today, the doctors say her condition is 'guarded' and it is too early to make any kind of prognosis. The heart infection is the first thing to 'fix' and the regimen is pencillin for 4 weeks, the ID doctor prefers six, but they will be monitoring, so once it is gone, we can start addressing the leaky heart valve. No point in putting in new valve to get contaminated.

Continue to pray, I'm not promising to post any updates here, but know this will be a long road to recovery for Kathi. Thank you. If you want to know anything, please call me. Try to curtail your emails, messenger and texts to Kathi, she is pretty much unconscious and will not be responding and I will not necessarily be monitoring two phones, Facebook timelines, or the like. If you require a response or want to know about Kathi; contact me. As long as she is in ICU, no flowers. If you have flowers place them in front of Our Lady for Kathi and light a candle. Oh and if you come visit her in the hospital; NO PIX! Especially on FB. Respect her privacy and current state of vulnerability. I'm surprised I have to say that.

September 30, 2014.

Dr. A. came by, very concerned about Kathi's heart and badly leaking mitral valve. He asked if Dr. G., the cardio-thoracic surgeon had come by yet; no. I asked Dr. A. about the labs he had requested last week, particularly the two he requested when he heard about Kathi's dad dying from Amyloidosis. He said they were of no consequence right now, but that the labs had not come back yet. We're making progress. Kathi kept fighting to get that tube out as she was waking up and finally succeeded even with her hands strapped down. She waited until housekeeping run us out of the room and she did it, drawing her body to her strapped down hands.

The night nurse said that Kathi is probably taking longer because her kidneys are not operating at full capacity yet, so not filtering as quickly.

October 1, 2014.

I write because I hurt. I guess this is what Todd Rundgren meant by the "Tortured Artist Effect"[19]. My love for Kathi has selfishly blinded my vision. I have been blind to what her eyes have been telling me and the misunderstanding of what her action in extubating herself meant yesterday. Since they were in the weaning process anyway, they allowed Kathi to breathe on her own and she managed until 2:30 this morning, before they had to re-intubate her, this was 12 hours! She wants no more suffering and we are only prolonging that inexplicable suffering.

Yesterday her body was shaking the bed from the labored breathing and her mile a minute heart beat. It is the body's natural instinct to strive for that last breath and the next one. Yet, that is the entire reason Kathi told me to call the EMS last Wednesday, she couldn't catch her breath. And no matter how good Dr. Ga. fixes her heart; Drs. G., D., L.D., S and F, will not fix her ability to breathe easier.

The MAC/MAI, bronchiectasis and pseudonymous are working together to suffocate her.

Has she suffered enough Jesus? Will/is her suffering serving as penance for her or some other family member? Who am I to have that say? Only know that she is suffering and Dr. G. told us in July that she will continue to suffer through the end of her life. When will that be?

And how do I make that call? My entire being screams against that responsibility, because it is not mine to make. So how do I approach this today? I will tell Kathi, I finally recognize what her eyes have been telling me and I have been selfishly ignoring them. This is not exactly how this train of thought started, but where it led. Kathi was sedated and docile (resting) most of the day.

11:30 PM; in Kathi's ICU room. Now, they think she aspirated and there appears to be something in her right lung, which they are treating for, with a more generic antibiotic; Zoxycin/Zopyicin? And have curtailed the penicillin for now. What more can she take? Again, God, I ask you, to what grand purpose/mystery does her suffering serve? Why did you allow her to come back (twice, so far)?

October 2, 2014.

They will be doing tracheostomy on Kathi tomorrow mid-morning (dependent upon the schedules of the specialists involved), the sooner the better and will be better for her versus the ventilator. The Zosyn is stronger than penicillin and attacks the streptococcus too. It was administered because ID doctor thought she might have pneumonia; but the cultures are not indicating pneumonia. They'll know more tomorrow when they perform the trach and do some more culture gathering. If they do not see pneumonia/pus, they will put her back on penicillin, because it does not have the side effects that zosyn does.

They've got her hands strapped down again, she was yanking on the tube throughout the night. The trach will be beneficial because it will allow her lungs to 'dry' out more, the tube won't be in her mouth and hopefully she'll be able to communicate/talk and 'if' she yanks out the trach tube, it's a 'simple' matter of reconnecting it.

Dr. S was discussing Kathi's conditions, even the potential for an acute/emergency heart valve replacement before the streptococcus is killed, however, she would not make it through any surgery at this time. Dr. S is not making any calls, Kathi's condition is still guarded, but outlook is grim, with so many things in play.

I also met with Dr. F (ID doctor) and Dr. L (cardiologist). These are the meetings I have been anticipating based on Kathi's physical condition, her spiritual condition is ready to move on. She is done with the suffering and her suffering will continue with her lungs even if they are successful with the minimally invasive heart valve replacement. I'm pretty sure that is primary reason she pulled out the tube, aside from its discomfort – it was in her eyes. They are talking about perhaps doing that soon as soon as they can get Kathi in a 'stable' condition and they may have to do it anyway considering the risks and her surviving any kind of surgery are very low. Even before they start the necessary heart surgery, they have to prep her with a heart catherization, which carries its own risks relative to the dye which is very toxic and since her kidneys are not functioning at full capacity, things could go south even before any incision is made. The cardio-thoracic surgeon has already weighed in; he will not do the surgery on her at this time as it will be 100% unsuccessful. The only organ in Kathi that is not impacted is her brain.

The fluid on her lungs is indicative of pneumonia (they'll know more tomorrow when they do the tracheostomy, and get more samples of the inside of her lungs) and congestive heart failure.

Please pass on to any family/friends which are not on this email list. If you have not seen Kathi, now would be the time.

October 3, 2014.

Kathi looks very sunken today, her eyes are sunken and dark, it is her whole appearance, it looks like the bed is consuming her. The tracheostomy went well and she was under anesthesia for about 4 hours. When she awoke and saw Ian and me, she got a big, bright smile which showed all her beautiful teeth.

Then the parade of visitors began and she tried to talk, but still cannot. Ian brought a letter board he uses for his children and there were three 'translators' who were arguing amongst themselves, plus I do not think Kathi's synapse in her brain are working exactly right as the words she is spelling out are not words.

She lasted about 5 minutes without the ventilator. They plugged her back in, will try again this week-end.

Oct 4, 2014.

I finally had to shut down the parade. It was becoming too much for Kathi. She even pointed to the door for her sister-in-law. I sent out the edict. Kathi's heart rate, blood pressure and respiratory rate accelerated and she could not control even though I tried to elicit/resurrect our Lamaze breathing practices (that is reaching back thirty-five years!). She was given some calming meds and she rested the rest of the day. She asked me if she was going to make it and I told her yes.

Oct 5, 2014 5:30 PM:

Kathi has asked that I write and she wants me to do it standing up, which is a trick. I think we're not communicating. She just told me to hurry up. She had another exciting day as they attempted to put in a pic line in both arms. They could not install in the left, so then they tried the right and it didn't go all the way either, kind of bent like a fish hook, the pic nurse said 'maybe' it will work itself out using blood flow as the rationale.

Kind of tough for Kathi's typical low blood flow/pressure. I'm not sure what she wants me to write, but she wants me to write as an advocate. Now she has gas and wants me to do something.

She was not successful again in being off the ventilator, lasted about 5 minutes before she was gasping for air, which does not help her demeanor. It takes her a long time to calm down.

October 6, 2014.

I was thinking this morning about the fish hook. How will the blood flow straighten it out, if Kathi is already experiencing low blood flow, exacerbated by her badly leaking mitral valve? This is a question for the doctors. Another question popped in my head, since they seem to be doing X-rays and CT scans practically daily on Kathi. I called Dr. L.D.'s office about the results of Kathi's lung CT scan, which occurred on September 12. 'Sonia' informed me they have not received yet! So much for ASAP!

October 7, 2014.

More concern. Kathi has contracted a fungus in her lungs and the antibiotic treatment has a side effect of arrhythmia. Dr. S tells me this morning we are rapidly approaching a convergent point, walking on a tightrope, balancing act. Tweak here, we fall on this side, tweak there, we fall on the other side. Now, we're going to slowly wean Kathi off the ventilator by end of week to see how she handles it. He said most patients handle it within 8 hours of the tracheostomy. But, that is my Kathi, she is not like most, she is special.

October 8, 2014.

Dr. A. is going to schedule group meeting to address path forward. It sounds like decision time for me and all the doctors. Today Fr. Mauricio and I celebrated a private Mass in Kathi's ICU room and she received Holy Communion! Praise God!

October 9, 2014.

Kathi is still here in ICU, 2 weeks and a day, so far, no end in sight, as the doctors battle Kathi's ailments on all fronts. There appears to be no magic wand and I have no answers. Dr. A. wants all doctors to meet with the family – waiting on alignments of schedules/calendar. I prayed with the gift of tears this morning for about 2 hours.

I am too tired at the end of the day to reflect or even pray. I feel I am doing Kathi a disservice and not ministering to her – being a deacon after all! "A man is not recognized in his own country".

Kathi is a little more coherent today, she has 'boxing gloves' on. I suppose she's a danger to herself yanking out her tubes. If Dr. A. came by this morning, I missed him, I had trouble sleeping, switching beds, after getting home last night at 11:30, with a little break from 8:30 -10:30 to eat supper. I prayed for a couple of hours this morning, but in terms of getting over here to the hospital, I just could not get going.

Kathi is not a balancing act. The doctors' approach and course of treatment(s) considering all her other issues and the treatment takes her to the other side of the happy medium. Then the doctors have to readjust the treatment, which takes her back over the medium and balance line. The doctors are in a constant battle, while it seems they are losing grasp.

Do not get me wrong, the doctors, nurses and staff are making vigilant, valiant efforts, but at times, seem overwhelmed by what Kathi presents them, I know I am. I hold her previous specialists responsible for this current situation. They missed information they had available to them, even an echocardiogram apparently last done in 2011, which reflected a leaky mitral valve. No echocardiograms since.

At 9:20, Dr. S turned down her ventilator setting to 6; slowly weaning her down to try and take her off the ventilator sometime this week-end, and if she has trouble give her oxygen.

At 7:00 PM, Our daughter wanted to visit mama by herself, I came back because Kathi got spooled up again, which took two hours to get her calmed down again.

October 10, 2014.

So, today I visited with the infectious disease doctor; his part is going 'well'. Cardiologist and surgeon say Kathi is not capable of undergoing surgery of any kind at this time. The lead doctor recommended she be put in something called a LTAC; Long Term Acute Care Facility, they are experienced at weaning patients off ventilators and Kathi can complete the full 6 week penicillin there. He also said there is no guarantee that Kathi will be strong enough at the end of the regimen to undergo surgery or ever. And at some time, we will have to begin addressing End of Life issues!

At 5:30 PM, Kathi began her daily anxiety bout, but does not seem bad yet at 6:05. At 6:10 she has a fever and they gave her Tylenol.

Oct 11, 2014

Kathi was agitated again last night. I finally figured out that is her 'awake' time. In the mornings, she is pretty much in lala land, in the late afternoon/evening, she being a night owl comes into her element. Last night she was telling me she saw her sister (she had passed away a year earlier from pancreatic cancer),–I told her not to listen to her sister, that she was a lost and wandering soul. Then Kathi said she saw butter-flies, when I asked what kind, she said 'bad', so I proceeded to douse the room with Holy Water and "by the blood of Jesus, I cast you out!".

Then Kathi told me she saw pretty birds. I told her they were angels. Some of this, I ascribe to the meds and her general altered state (the door has been opened). However, because of my faith and what I have witnessed in the past, I am leaving nothing to circumspect.

Now there are suspect fungals (2 different) living in her lungs. Really?!? Something is really determined to kill her. End of life dis-cussion with doctors to come. She is still very much aware and awake – she is not an animal; I will not make her comfortable!

I finally remembered that the day before she entered the hospital, when Kathi had an appointment with her PCP, who diagnosed among many things, something called Involuntary Familial or Essential Tremors. I let the attending doctors and nurses know this as they thought Kathi was spending her entire living moments attempting to pull out the breathing tube. She was not necessarily doing it on purpose.

I met with Dr. S, who says there are indications of 2 fungals in her lungs, they do not know if they are the colonizing type or just dormant, (see fever from yesterday and she still has low grade fever) parenthesis – author's emphasis.

PCP's associate says there is no change, she needs to go to LTAC, truly long-term acute care. I told him to let PCP know that my schedule is clear to meet with doctors for team meeting.

Congestive heart failure is continuing to flood her lungs. It's a circle jerk, only Kathi is the brunt of the cosmic joke. Kathi was weaker yesterday and weaker still today. Is it because of the two fungi now living in her lungs? Dyspnea/Aemoptysis – shortness of breath – Duh!?!

Kathi asked me this morning where she was; this is a daily event. Dr. S said the new lasics is working much better.

6:10 PM.

She has not really come around this day. Her tremors keep drawing her hands up into the fetal position. She is barely moving her mouth to 'talk'; no strength, very weak. Slept all day. Forty years ago, I had premonition of pending death on Sunday November 9. I thought at the time, it was my death and it still may very well be as I looked ahead on the calendar and sure enough, November 9 falls on a Sunday this year.

I guess I looked because of Kathi's current condition. Two years ago, I thought we would be celebrating Christmas without Kathi's sister. It may be for this year without Kathi. It is very difficult to keep up the face of hope and faith in this environment. Now it sounds like she is wheezing.

October 12, 2014.

Kathi, to me, seems to be getting worse, she told me last night that she didn't want to be like this and wanted to go. She is less and less responsive, she at least stuck out her tongue at the nurse this morning. She keeps trying to get up and talk to someone I can't see and she is unable to tell me who it is. Her jaw is relaxed and she is drooling, I suctioned it and she was aware of the swab when I gave her water. I think she is in transition; her physical body is in final stages of shutting down. Her spiritual self is trying to leave, but the body has not released her yet.

October 13, 2014.

My insurance does not cover the LTAC I was interested in touring in New Braunfels. In fact my insurance only covers one of the dozen or so in the area; LifeCare. No sedation today for Kathi, she was feisty for four hours today; told me to shut up and blah, blah, blah. She's tired in the PM and didn't like the ski boots. I sat her up in a more upright position. We prayed the Rosary at 3:00 PM today and she held PawPaw's (OG) Rosary.

Her heart rate is running a little high, still has low grade fever. I visited the LTAC facility, talked and toured with Claudia. Place seems nice enough, parking is much better, it's a 72 bed, one floor facility.

October 14, 2014.

Kathi sat up in the bed today, and the nurse transformed the bed into a chair, Kathi's feet touched the floor for the first time in 3 weeks. Kathi had her first BM, it's like when you have a baby, you get so excited when they have their first one. Kathi was moved to LifeCare this evening, not a good first experience. Our daughter and I had to wait for 'visiting hours'. So we went down the street to Luby's for dinner. Then we came back for the final visiting hours of the day; 8:00 to 9:00 PM, got there, Kathi is in ICU-2 and Nurse Daniel was misinformed. My daughter and I got them straightened out, ensuring she got her meds, before we left. Apparently, the turnover package was lacking.

October 15, 2014.

Going to LifeCare now, it's a 20 mile drive from the house, versus basically across the highway, let's see what the day holds. Patient in ICU-1 coded; no doctor, continued CPR for 20 minutes, finally made the call. A little while later, gurney covering body in purple blanket rolls out to the mortuary van.

Kathi is prescribed Lopressor for her BP, but they have to monitor closely, since it affects her heart rate, which is being 'controlled' by propofol. The acute care specialist (PCP counterpart) came to see Kathi. There is no cardiologist making rounds; on call, if we need one? After explaining Kathi's condition to the good doctor, she realized and said they are used to having a cardiologist make rounds for other patients – he keeps all hours of the day and night and usually comes by sometime between 9:00 PM and 5:00 AM. While talking to the doctor, I remembered that some of the meds Kathi was taking were being administered orally.

The ID doctor as a matter of technique is switching Kathi's meds, dropping the 'zole'.

Kathi will have low grade fevers based on all her other underlying conditions, particularly her lungs. The fungi live there and as a result of being in the air. Her MAC/MAI is an outgrowth of her bronchiectasis. Well, that's news.

Kathi was visited and evaluated today by her nurse, respiratory therapy (RT), occupational therapy (OT), physical therapy (PT) and speech therapy (ST). She also received a bath, they washed her hair and Kathi experienced another BM. Kathi's respirator kept popping off, not Kathi pulling it off. Therapist finally fixed it at 3:30 PM.

October 16, 2014.

Kathi was visited by cardiologist, who changed her heart medicine, and she was visited by the OT/PT doctor. Kathi had a 15 minute workout and another bath.

October 17, 2014.

I had to be at one of my clients facility today, while finishing up a project and at 3:30 PM, I received a call from the Case Manager, to discuss initial planning and End of Life (EOL). I arrived at LifeCare at 4:30 PM, kind of tough to cross town during that time of day. Kathi was agitated, breathing spiked up to 70 bpm. Nurse came in at 5:30 pm surprised to see her awake. Respiratory Therapist (RT) came in to check on Kathi's breathing, set oxygen to 100% and changed the inline filter.

Kathi was visited by pulmonologist from a group; they rotate rounds every week. And her 'new' cardiologist came by at 6:30 PM, and drew me a couple of sketches of Kathi's heart, as shown below in Figures 1017-1 and 1017-2. He explained to me that it was a long 5 step surgical process and that both cannot be accomplished in the same surgery:

1. First, get rid of the infection
2. Work on her lungs
3. Work on her strength
4. Replace mitral valve
5. Then fix hole, which is done with some sort of double umbrella stint

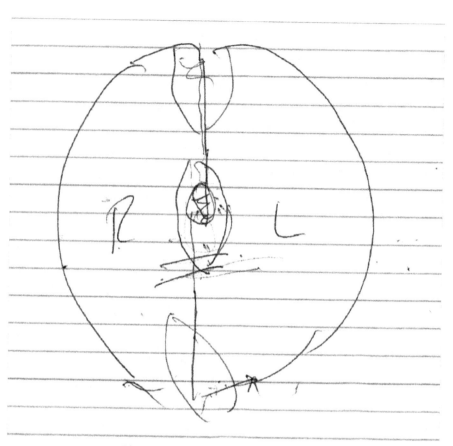

Figure 1017-1. Rough Heart Diagram.

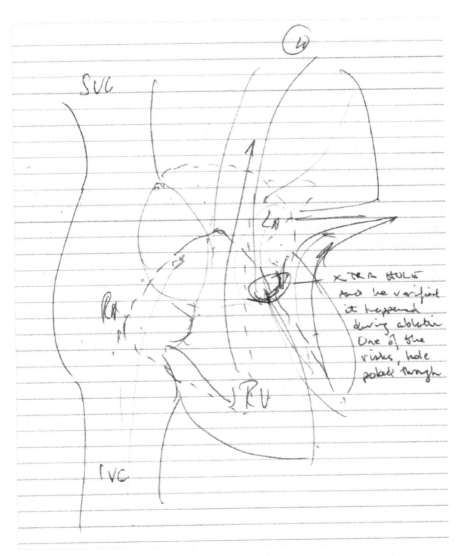

Figure 1017-2. Rough Diagram of Kathi's Heart. Sketch shows approximate area where the ablation procedure caused hole is in Kathi's heart.

He explained to me that not only does she have the badly leaking mitral valve, but she also has a hole in her septum that was caused by an ablation procedure. I told him two things:

1. The hole in her septum occurred in April ablation, cardiologist was not aware she had had two ablations and I had told the electrophysiologist at the time, he had taken the life out of her. Unfortunately, that is one of the risks associated with the ablation procedure.

2. I was a little upset that the doctors at the first hospital had not informed me of the second hole in her heart. Now, I know why, the cardiologists from the electrophysiologist group were so reserved; particularly the one who had admitted her to the hospital in late July – he actually appeared afraid, when I reminded him, yes, I remember you, you admitted Kathi to the Cardiac Short Stay hospital the last weekend of July.

The cardiologist went on to explain to me that badly leaking mitral valve and the extra hole in her heart have a side effect of causing scar tissue in the lungs – Oh Great!?!?

Author's emphasis, it appears the first hospital may have washed their hands.

October 18, 2014.

I had a tough time going to see Kathi today. I asked Kathi's BFF to go sit with Kathi today, but I did not get much 'rest' from all the texts and phone calls from her BFF; just helping Kathi build up a head of steam.

I arrived at about 4:10 PM and Kathi was resting peacefully, so I went back out to main waiting room. I checked on her a couple of times and found her awake at 5:10 PM. She was awake and naturally very agitated because she had had a BM and no one was checking on her. I located one of the staff (Kathi's assigned nurse for the day) who was hunkered down in the staff break room and of course, I had entered 'hallowed ground' by crossing the imaginary HIPPA line to access her. No big deal for me, I've crossed union lines in the past to get product to the customer. In this instance, the customer required assistance and I went in search of that assistance, since I'm not qualified to provide that assistance.

Later, this same nurse said she was keeping score of Kathi's BMs and even went so far as posting them on the whiteboard in Kathi's room. Really? Trying to 'shame' her? Later, as this nurse was attending to Kathi (whose hands were restrained), she called Kathi 'princess' in a derogatory manner – I believe the princess was the attendant, who seems to have the wrong altitude for someone in the healthcare profession (author's perspective).

I stayed until about 9:30 PM (another HIPPA violation!). Kathi was resting peacefully and I told her earlier that her bpm were lower than yesterday (a good thing) and stable like her HR and BP.

October 19, 2014.

Doctors and I never met. Kathi is now at a long term acute care facility called LifeCare, the only one covered by my insurance, the privilege I receive at $20,000.00 a year. The upside is that the facility is about five minutes from my son and his family's house.

I think that I am beginning to empathize with those who suffer debilitating depression, I am unable/unwilling to move or do anything, I am paralyzed, and everything seems like a chore. God forbid, if she dies. Which it seems the medical profession has ensured that through negligence.

Again, I asked Kathi's BFF to sit with Kathi as I intended to serve at Masses today, however, I am just not ready to face the Masses. One of Kathi's aunts called me this morning to see if it was okay for her and her daughter (Kathi's cousin) to visit. I said no, but later recanted and left her aunt a voicemail in the affirmative. I texted my son to release the hordes and I texted my daughter to see if she wanted to go see her mama. I may go to the 5:30 PM Mass or look for a Mass near the house, where no one knows me.

Ok, so maybe my goal of an email every night was a little aggressive in retrospect. I apologize for not keeping up with it, but I will try to going forward. Anyway, some good stuff has happened. Kathi's aunt and cousin came by and prayed with practicing yoga meditations bringing Kathi calm and peace. That lasted about 8 minutes as a doctor came in hollering; "How ya doin today?". (I'm in ICU, how do you think I'm doing; numbnuts?"). Another thing is that she has started to feel more (in fact all of her senses seem to be a bit stronger). This is a double edged sword though. On one hand she feels chest/heart/throat pain more than before, but on the other hand she can control herself more which leads me to the fact that she wrote today (a lot) to ask for things, ask questions, and the like. She can communicate again which is incredibly good for her. I stayed until 10:45 P.M., I felt bad for the night guard as he would have to come around from the counter and through various doors to unlock the main door to let me out.

October 20, 2014.

I got to bed about midnight, then woke up at 3:30, did some work for about 3 hours. I then launched into mindless chores around the house; cleaning up, sorting/putting away bills, catching up on mundane stuff. I took a couple of naps.

I met with the Case Manager from 4:00 to 5:00 PM about Kathi moving to a longer long-term care (not acute; nursing home/hospice) facility. I thought we were already in a long term acute care facility? I recognize Kathi will be in some sort of 'care' (now I use this term loosely) facility through Christmas, most likely longer. I stayed through 'report', then left for the evening, once I was comfortable with next shift.

October 21, 2014.

And PLEASE when you talk to Kathi, be a message of love, hope and peace. Do not discuss with her how long she is going to be there; that does not aid in the healing process. Put yourself in her place (if you can) and consider having pretty much lost the last six months of your life, you probably have that much more to 'look' forward to, spending Thanksgiving, Christmas, maybe your birthday in the hospital and not being able to see or play with your grandkids. Again, be a messenger of love, hope, comfort, peace and prayer.

Do you think I need to add this? It came to me after I read your email, turned off the computer and was getting ready to go to work. I know people, some of them say things they don't think about as conversation starters.

Kathi asked her brother where I was and she wanted to see me. I put in four hours at one of my client's facilities. I got to LifeCare about 1:45 P.M. and OT/PT had just finished putting Kathi in a fancy chair. She wanted to stay sitting in it for an hour and she did! They're putting her back in her bed now (~ 3:00 PM). Tomorrow, they are going to put in a stomach peg (J-PEG – not image) at 2:00 PM to replace her NG Tube. *Percutaneous endoscopic gastrojejunostomy (PEG-J) is performed in patients who cannot receive food into the stomach and, thus, have to be fed via the small intestine. In this procedure, a standard PEG tube is placed, and then a smaller tube (a jejunal tube) is placed through the PEG tube and positioned down into the small intestine.*[20]

October 22, 2014.

This event has challenged and shown me just how weak my faith is; my prayers are half-hearted, seem rote, even though I'm not saying any written prayers other than the Rosary and the Lord's Prayer. I say half-hearted because after all this time, I still do not know what is in my heart. I have been paralyzed in attending Church, much less serving as Deacon, my heart has not been in it and I have not wanted to face the hordes at Mass – even though deep down I know those hordes at our parish are concerned because they love us – well more that they love Kathi, I'm just a conduit to her. Their prayers are working beyond my weak faith. Are my tears prayers? Then I have been praying.

Kathi is making a miraculous and slow recovery. She is improving, gaining strength, which is what she needs to do in order to undergo the necessary/required heart surgery replacing her mitral valve; even her involuntary tremors appear to be decreasing. She is having the peg put in right now on schedule. This will replace the feeding tube in her nose and make her much happier.

Even today, she asked me if she was going to make it. I told her yes, based on the positive progress she has been making, she will be going home. She will teach our two young grandsons how to swim.

Today's Gospel Luke 12: 39-48 spoke to me and reminded me that my life is not my own. It's time to move out of the personal pity party and live as a Christian. Kathi is suffering and we suffer together in our Baptism with Jesus Christ.

October 23, 2014.

Good Afternoon,

I just wanted to drop everyone a line and let them know that there have been a few developments and though they seem minor, they bring great joy. As I said before, Kathi has been able to start writing and her handwriting has gotten a lot better (it doesn't look like mine anymore). This is mainly because she has been gaining some strength and her involuntary tremors have really subsided. In addition to that, she has been able to become a lot more expressive, non-vocally, which really helps in interpreting what she is mouthing. This extra strength and control also lets her do things for herself like brush her hair, she got a big BIG smile out of that.

Lastly, one of her biggest discomforts has been the feeding tube in her nose, but that has been removed since they have installed a stomach peg to feed her that way.

Despite these strides, she is still obviously recovering, and will continue to do so for quite a while. With that being said, family are still welcome, and as always, please be a calming influence, only come two at a time and, of course, no kids (our grand- kids have really started to ask about their GaGa), pets, flowers, or plants and if she is asleep, it's because she needs it and let her sleep.

Thank you so much for your love, prayers and support.

October 24, 2014.

This has been quite a morning! Kathi stood up for 15 minutes, brushed her teeth and got her own ice chips from a cup, breathed on her own for two hours with a CPAP. Praise God!

From this afternoon through Sunday October 26, 2014, I have enlisted support from family and friends to kind of sit with and be with Kathi. One of Kathi's aunts had put together a rotating schedule to go and hang out with Kathi, which included all of the "sisters", her brother and our son. This week-end is our annual co-owners meeting in Port Aransas, Texas where Kathi and I are blessed to own a condo. No, you do not have to feel sorry for me and that is not the reason for this entry. But, I did make the decision last week-end to attend, I felt that I needed it, recognizing that Kathi's recovery was a long haul and she was not ready for the required mitral valve replacement yet. And God Bless Her, with everything facing her, Kathi told me to go. So, with much trepidation this afternoon, a Friday, kind of staying within routine for that, I will get on southbound 281 and attempt to get to the coast, putting the truck on cruise control at the posted speed limit and try to enjoy the sunset in our other backyard. When Kathi and I go to our place on the coast, this is one of the highlights, for us anyway, to watch the sunsets while we are there. There is no schedule; we usually eat supper European style, so that it does not interfere with our watching the sunset. There have been times, we have stepped out on a limb and actually packed a meal to sit on the beach or at least a snack of wine, cheese and crackers.

I packed food/meals for this trip and planned to barbeque Saturday evening, since the pit is right outside our back door. I arrived in time for sunset, but upon opening the door recognized the condo had not been cleaned, since Kathi's aunts had been here for the Hummingbird Festival the previous month. I set about stripping all the beds and gathering the dirty towels and putting them all in clothes basket. The plan being to go to the laundromat in the morning. Fortunately, we keep extra towels, sheets, pillow cases and the like and I remade the master bed. I'm a man so just because what I put on there was bigger than the bed did not matter, it kept me off the mattress and would come off when I left on Sunday anyway. Our housekeeper recently began having her own health issues and was unable to clean for us. Then I visited with our coastal next door neighbor, Ms. Betty and got caught up with her and some of the other neighbors; as Betty was hosting a margarita party on her back porch. She invited me and I enjoyed the company, even though all we talked about was Kathi's health and a little about our concerns with the management company. At dusk, I thanked Betty for the invite and told her I would be around through Sunday, maybe Monday (little did I know). I went into my place and prepared my supper, asked for blessing of my meal, washed the dishes and went back out on the back porch to enjoy the evening air. I took my ipod and the portable speakers to listen to music, again kind of a tradition that both Kathi and I enjoy. As the evening wore on, it became very apparent on my soul that I was very lonely and I experienced my gift of tears over the past few months; I allowed for a personal pity party.

October 25, 2014. Gommie's birthday.

I awoke this morning, made coffee and prayed the morning office. I walked down to the beach to greet the sunrise and took about a 4 mile walk, first east toward town, then west past our condos and back. As I took this walk, it reminded me that I have wanted to do 'something' about the litter on my beach, but at this moment, all I did was think about it and the first beach house we stayed at on our Hawaii trip in June. The owners of that beach house, had collected debris from the beach and sorted them by color into four large clear plastic jars and placed them on a display rack in the house. It was a kind of 'art', but also served as a reminder of what we as a species are doing to this planet we call home. I have these two wagons stored at the condo, which I could pull behind me on my walks and pick up the litter, bring it back to the condo and sort it perhaps in this same style of urban art. Maybe next time.

From the morning walk, I came back and ate breakfast, piled the dirty clothes into the truck and dropped the baskets of clothes at the laundromat, they would be done in a couple of hours. You didn't think I was going to wash the clothes did you? I ran some errands around town, picked up cleaning supplies, got back to the condo and cleaned it. About the time I finished, it was time for the meeting, went there, listened to the reports and news, they fed us lunch, I visited with the management company representative and other co-owners. I left the meeting, drove over to the laundromat, picked up the wrapped bundles of clean sheets, pillowcases and towels, and returned to the condo. Then, in the midafternoon, I felt it was a time to write, I got the materials, plus my music box and assumed the position on my back porch.

I barbequed a small ribeye steak and made a salad for supper, a front is coming in, it sure is windy. I'm imbibing a beer as is the tradition. Unfortunately, Kathi is not sitting here with me on the picnic table at the gazebo; it's just me. And my construction site radio has finally seen too many days at the beach; it no longer works, the outside is corroded, I'm sure the interior components (the important parts) are corroded as well. I'll put that on the list for the next trip down, in addition to a new vacuum cleaner to clean the tile floors. I do not know where all this sand comes from.

October 26, 2014.

I woke up, prayed the morning office and read today's readings. I packed the truck and intend to go home after breakfast. I'm excited to be going to Mass at St. Joseph's and enjoying Father Kris' homily. As always, his homilies are timely and relevant and without notes, except for the ones in/from his heart. Hopefully, I will someday be blessed with that capability.

Now, just a left turn then the next right and I'll be parking at the Island Diner for my Sunday breakfast. It did not take me very long to realize this week-end, that perhaps I cannot be here by myself, without Kathi. That is why I'm going home today, I had planned in the back of my head to perhaps stay until Monday. I guess I will sell the place if she does not leave the hospital; I've already told everyone I'm not messing with 'sharing' it, because that is what Kathi does and she is in the hospital, so the condo sits vacant and un/under appreciated. It's a travesty.

I arrived home and went straight to the hospital. Even though her aunt had set up a schedule for familial and friend support, few kept to the schedule, if at all. Partially, perhaps or just because of Kathi's health, she had a rough and restless week-end. She was very tired, frustrated and somewhat confused about what happened to her and told everyone to stay away. She was glad to see me.

She told me about a couple of dreams/visions she had. The first one involved an old priest who performed tracheostomy on Kathi at a church. The second one was that she was in a hospital in Nova Scotia, which was across the street from an ice house (convenience store) and that I was concerned about an 18 wheeler of beer (Bud Light, no less!) and I left to go get and drive the semi somewhere else and I was inviting

105

everyone to the party. Kathi was very agitated with me (in the dream, of course!).

Kathi seemed to be a bit better, but is just frustrated by her situation. She looks good, but she misses her grandkids (they miss her too), she misses her own bed, and of course she has an idea of how long she'll be there so she's not looking forward to that. She did mention that she was very happy to see everyone (despite cancelling some of the visits) and specifically mentioned that she enjoyed her Aunt Dottie's stories today. Thank you to everyone who volunteered and to aunt Helen for setting it up.

On a brighter note, she can talk! This is great for her!! Buuuuuut, she's not supposed to try to talk with the tracheotomy in–lol. How successful does everyone think we are at getting her to write everything down now that she can talk? Right, not very. Additionally, she is able to stand on her own (though she still needs help standing up). This is not something that she can do all the time, or for long periods, but she was able to stand up for 15 minutes and brush her teeth.

October 27, 2014.

Kathi's j-peg is hurting worse. They did a CT scan of the area, the doctor who performed the procedure reviewed the scan, came in and told Kathi (and me) two things; (1) he did not realize that Kathi's liver stretched all the way to that side and (2) he thinks he may have perforated the tip of her liver. Explaining that the liver itself has no feeling, but has a film around it which is sensitive and the j-peg tube is probably rubbing against the 'film' causing the pain. So they are going to have a do-over tomorrow.

Earlier today, they sent in a psychiatrist because they thought Kathi may be experiencing anxiety keeping her from weaning from the ventilator. Are you kidding me??? I wish he would have come after if he wanted to see some anxiety! Kathi was very agitated today, when I first got here.

October 28, 2014.

There was excitement today. Ants! Last night, Kathi said she woke up and her right elbow was covered by ants in the her bed. The nurses said she was hallucinating. When I got there, there were ants all along all three sides of the floor of her room. I got a nurses and a doctor's attention and showed them the ants, they summoned facilities and they did what they could in an ICU area relative to bug spray. Kathi certainly has a vivid imagination!

Her pulmonologist, or at least the one making the rounds this week, began decreasing the ventilator setting to start the weaning process again and put Kathi on CPAP at 9:30 A.M. At 11:00 A.M., the speech therapist performed a swallow test with a scanning machine, which included a barium dye.

I realized that the doctors were not reading the charts, only what applied to their specialty. I learned this lesson twenty years ago, when we almost lost our daughter. I mentioned this to the house doctor about communication and coordination and she was not overly concerned; it was up to the individual doctors to read the charts and make their decisions relative to the information contained within. I also asked about how often Kathis vitals were being observed and I mentioned the automated BP check is set for once an hour, when at the other hospital ICU, it was set to read BP every 15 minutes or quarter hour. The doctor then mentioned to me, that if Kathi were in the general hospital part of this rehab facility, they would only check her vitals every four hours, again not concerned about her BP status. I mentioned Kathi's BP reading I remembered from yesterday's readings: 95/54, 83/58, 72/30 and 85/31. She said there was no concern over the diastolic reading, I said "Okay, doc, thank you for your time". I'm in dire straits.

12:30 PM

Good News! They're removing her j-peg, the pulmonologist made the call, said she does not need it since she is swallowing alright. Bad news, or maybe it was a mixed blessing (easy for me to say) they punctured her liver when they put it in and that's what was causing the pain. I guess if she hadn't been in so much pain and complaining – they wouldn't have taken the steps or considered leaving the tube out, outright! Good news, course if they're taking out and leaving the tube out; how's she going to get nutrition? Through mechanical soft food – that's how! She gets to eat!

And better news; the Cardiologist said the infection is gone today, four weeks to the day after starting the antibiotic! However, they are taking it to the full six weeks. Praise God!

October 29, 2014.

So this week has been one of pretty darn good news. As I told everyone before, the stomach j-peg feeding tube was put in so that they could take out the NG feeding tube. As days went by it began hurting more and more, after complaining enough, they did a CT scan and found out that they pierced her liver when putting it in! (I began imagining that all of her doctors were in that Benny Hill chase scene). Anyway, they removed it and decided that she was at a point that she could begin eating real food. She is incredibly happy about that. Today's meal looked like beef stroganoff (a real meal).

October 30, 2014.

Kathi started to learn how to speak around the trach early in the week, then today they put a "speaking cap" on the trach and now she fully has her own voice back. She called me from Ms. Vicki's phone and left a voicemail; what a sweet sound! With that being said, she wants visitors! Family and friends, come one, come all. The hospital rules only allow two visitors at a time, so we must abide by that, however she is feeling better.

So, not only are these smaller things happening, but 4 weeks to the day after she began her antibiotic regimen, her heart infection is gone! She is getting stronger too, she was able to get up and walk today! These are all great things!

Thank you everyone for your love and support, we still have a ways to go but there are many positives at this time. Of course, it still stands that if she is tired, please let her sleep. Still no kids, still no pets, still no flowers and still no plants.

October 31, 2014.

Sixteen years ago, I retired from the government. Retirement is a funny word. And today, my agreement with one of my biggest clients expires.

Kathi's creating quite a stir and I think 'they' want her out of this place. Plus, the ant debacle embarrassed the staff and left (imaginary) bites on Kathi's arms.

November 1, 2014.

Only the trach is attached to oxygen and Kathi gets very anxious about whether it is still connected and if she is getting enough oxygen. She also gets uncomfortable, which helps to exacerbate her anxiety. She can't find the right mix of pillows – I'm sure they call her the pillow lady. Plus, she has two little ones from the house. PT asked me to bring clothes from the house and I showed him the Barbie bag with panties, gym shorts, baseball jersey in her closet.

November 2, 2014.

Kathi was moved out of ICU to the general hospital portion of the rehab facility. I expressed my concern this evening about the lack of turnover communication/coordination between ICU and the hospital portion of LifeCare. I had to keep looking for the RT, and reminding her each time I located her, she was not finished setting up Kathi's oxygen in the new room. She even asked me what the setting was; I asked her, "Isnt that in Kathi's charts?". She was very irritated about something. Kathi's new room 316-1 is only 30 feet away from her ICU room through a set of double doors.

November 3, 2014. 5:30 PM

Kathi's out of ICU at the LTACF. She rode bicycle for 15 minutes today and sat in her chair for 4 hours. She 'lovingly' called her PT guy "bastard".

Staff was a little more attentive today, but my observation – who's looking out for those other patients like Kathi's roommate? I tried to do my part as I was raising heck for Kathi's care roaming the halls and standing at the nurse's station; I overheard the charge nurse on a telephone call with someone's family member. They were trying to find a priest for Kathi's roommate to provide the rite of Anointing of the Sick.

Being a deacon, I stuck my nose in and the nurse put me on the phone with the woman's daughter-in-law. I made some phone calls, then realized that all the priests in the Archdiocese were tied up with annual convocation conference. I left voicemails with several, but then got back in touch with the daughter-in-law and kept her apprised of the situation.

We had a new nurse today (literally, first day in the LifeCare System) after the two week orientation; course she has had good training at Brooke Army Medical Center (BAMC) and Wilford Hall. She was complaining about the bells and tones being different from other facilities where she worked in the past. During one of Kathi's resting periods, I got to know a little about her nurse, who told me where she got her start and training. She also informed me, since it was her first day, she had only been assigned two patients; both in the same room.

I'm getting tired of eating at Lubys. It reminds me of a place I used to work at as a teenager in the Midwest called Bishops, same kind of menu and format. I was a busboy, cook and dishwasher (not at the same time, I worked my way up to cook), so I know what goes on behind the doors.

I Forgot to mention that Kathi's 'new' nurse called me today to discuss administering medicine to my wife for low blood sugar – I was confused by the call and kept pressing her for more information and verifying that she was talking about my wife; Kathi in room 316; when I said that, she apologized, she had patients' confused and I told her I thought so, because I just met you and shook your hand in my wife's room. She continued to apologize. Before I left Kathi tonight, she was visited by one her aunts and a cousin and his wife, I told her roommate, who also had a trach and could not talk, I confused her somewhat, as her son's name is also Sean, that we were trying to get a priest in here to provide anointing of the sick for her. She mouthed "Thank you", to me. I understand that a priest came by later this evening.

November 4, 2014.

Kathi coded again last night, respiratory distress, cardiac arrest and CPR to bring her back, something about her trach being plugged according to Dr. F. I got the call at 5:26 A.M. When the nurse told me she coded, I asked her three times to repeat what she said. When I left last night, Kathi was resting and breathing peacefully.

Sitting in the lunch room today, I got to hear all about our new nurse's first day at LifeCare and her own medical history, as she dined/discussed with her workmates (5 others); to include a crass discussion of the 2 patients she was assigned to yesterday; one who kept complaining about pain near where her j-peg used to be, except in presence of doctor and the other one who was dying anyway.

I had half a mind to thank her for caring for my wife yesterday and that she should be more discreet in discussing her own medical history and the privacy of patients in her charge since one of her patients yesterday was my wife. But, I did not, because apparently, by listening to her trials, she has been given a second chance, by the same token, however her patients may be at risk due to her potential for flipping/ freaking out. I did not challenge her, simply because I was just tired.

November 8, 2014.

There isn't a whole lot to report right now. Kathi is back in ICU, however, she looks and acts as good as she did right before they moved her out of ICU. They don't have a clear answer as to what happened the other night, but they are monitoring her. She can't talk again because they switched out her trach away from the "talking trach", but she still has her dry erase board, body language, and can mouth words.

If you would like, you can go visit her again. She really seems strong again (or as strong as she has been recently), so I am sure that she would like to see some people. Hours for the ICU are 9-11, 12:30-2:30, 4:30-6:30, and 8-9. Please let me know if you have any questions.

November 9, 2014.

I served at several Masses today. The message is a call to Christian action, not just words, but deed as well, by example and activism. In today's Gospel of John; Jesus 'closes' the market in His Father's temple. It is not so much the exchanging of money and buying sacrificial animals as it is about the routineness we have become accustomed to, without considering the source of those 'motions'. Feed the poor, caring for the marginalized, widows and orphans, teaching the Good News to the ends of the earth! We seem to be more concerned with

'Black Friday' than defending the defenseless against injustice, harsh treatment, elderly abuse and neglect and abortion.

One of the parishioners leaving today, stopped and asked how Kathi was doing, I told her. Then, as sort of a confession, she told me she missed our Church. They had decided, for their children to attend a protestant church, because they (the children) enjoyed the youth program(s) of this other church. I did not ask her, but will later if I see her again, if she can relate to me; what draws her children and other children to the youth program of other denominations' churches versus what we offer?

Kathi did see me for a little while as she was sleeping when I came in and they had adjusted her ventilator from volume to pressure setting and she seems to be handling it better. However, she came around and felt the need for a BM, so I left while the nurses retrieved a bedpan. I gave them a ½ hour, because it takes her awhile and she gets out of breath from any little exertion. I gave them an extra 10 minutes and when I came back they were still attending to her and the nurse asked me to give them another 15 minutes as Kathi had become disconnected from the ventilator, experiencing shortness of breath and very anxious. I came back and she was knocked out, they gave her a sedative so she wouldn't be so agitated. Now it's supper time and she will miss what little nutrition she can get, because she'll be sleeping through the rest of the night probably. Even knocked out she is struggling for breath and she looks very pale. She looks like her mama and her gommie in the last days; trying to get what oxygen there is and like each breath is her last.

November 10, 2014.

The assistant from Dr. N's office in Austin, called to remind us of appointment tomorrow at 12:30. I politely told her I had cancelled the appointment two months ago and who I had talked to in her office. I also told her why I had cancelled the appointment.

Today must be the day. The assistant from Kathi's PCP office called reminding us of appointment on November 13. I let her know as well, that Kathi was in the hospital and that the PCP had already been visiting her everyday, up to three times a day.

I began working with the Case Manager in reviewing Advanced Directive (AD), Do Not Resuscitate (DNR) and Medical Power of Attorney (MPOA) documents. The Case Manager also came into Kathi's room to assist in explaining these three documents, pros and cons and their uses in patient care. And it appears these documents have slight variances from state to state depending on state's laws.

Kathi chose the MPOA authorizing me as her agent and our son, if I'm not available. This document basically states that if patient (Kathi) is unable to make decisions on her own, then I am legally allowed to make those medical decisions for her. It also requires an accompanying physician's letter stating that patient is unable and/or incapable to make her own decisions regarding her patient care.

November 11, 2014.

Today, Kathi told me of a dream/vision she had earlier in this journey. She was standing on the edge of a precipice and she was wearing cowboy boots, the one on her left foot was black and the one on her right was white. Also on her left was her deceased sister and on her right was our daughter. Her sister was telling her it was fine on 'this' side and to join her; our daughter was telling her all she had to do was move her right foot. Kathi said "I want to live" and moved her right foot forward. After that, she was awake in the ICU room.

November 12, 2014.

Kathi walked 20 feet today. She sat up in a chair for two hours, with a reduced ventilator assist.

November 15, 2014.

So yesterday, my brother-in-law comes to visit his sister, only thinking about his 'stuff'. He shares with us his last couple of days, how he had to go to some ribbon cutting/grand opening ceremony – because his business partners were sick – including his wife who was throwing up right before they went to the event. So, when I made a horrified comment and told him to leave the room, he said; "Oh, she's okay now!". No clue; why I was concerned about bringing another bug into an already dying person's room. And now, today apparently I have contracted the bug.

I was concerned about Kathi's heart rate yesterday (as she was, she could feel it); it was very erratic and noisy between beats and bouncing all over the place and she kept asking what her heart rate was on the monitor.

I thought I had something earthshattering to share today, I should've written it down when I thought it this morning. There are small joys in this life, which we miss; Kathi's smile and the honeybirds continuing to visit the feeders this time of year.

November 16, 2014.

I served at Mass today, one of the Masses was with our former priest, Monsignor Pat. To me this seemed to be a sign that everything would be alright. I continue to pray for this miracle.

Kathi's room has a window so she can see outside. The view is of two trees, one is a mesquite on a slight hill, which seems to have been caused by erosion because there is a dry bed between this hill and the building. Every day Kathi asks that the drapes be raised, so that she can see outside and watch the cardinals and sparrows go about their daily lives; today she got a surprise. Four of her five grandkids stood outside her window and held up big 'get well' posters they created and were waving frantically at their GaGa. My son was with his children and I put the speaker on my phone, so Kathi could hear her grandchildren's voices. This was very therapeutic.

November 18, 2014.

Today, Kathi and I 'celebrated' our 42nd Wedding Anniversary. I could not obtain my customary gift to her of the number of yellow roses representing our wedded years together; because there are no flowers/plants allowed in the ICU and I have no issue with that, which is a valid restriction for all the patients in the ward. But, Kathi was especially depressed and 'weepy' all day today, for the very reason that it was our wedding anniversary and she does not know how many more holidays, birthdays, graduations and anniversaries she is going to celebrate 'in here'. I did my best at trying to be there for her, consoling her, but her current status is overwhelming to her, so all I can do is hold her hand and pray. Sometimes, you just have to cry.

November 19, 2014.

The pulmonologist began discussing the 'plan'; Kathi was not going to get significantly better until she had the mitral valve replacement. The valve is leaking fluid back into the lungs. Kathi was all for it and mouthed "let's get this show on the road" and that she'd rather die on the operating table than waiting for that to happen in the ICU bed. Later, she wrote I want to live. So now we are waiting for the doctors and facilities to coordinate and communicate; personally, I feel they are trying to get her 'out of here' before Thanksgiving.

November 20, 2014.

Kathi walked 308 feet today in physical therapy! Everyone was beaming and high fiving. It sounds like the plan is to move Kathi to the main Methodist on Monday, they want to move her tomorrow, but there seems to be an issue with available beds in the Surgical ICU at the Methodist. In terms of familial communication, this is email our son sent out to the family and friends prayer distribution list.

Good Evening everyone!

I just wanted to write a quick note to everyone and let y'all know that if you would like to visit, now is the time because they are moving her to main Methodist on Monday to prepare her for surgery to replace her mitral valve! This is what we have been working towards for a while. She has gotten stronger each day, been able to walk further each day and has been on CPAP while awake for the last several days. We are not in the clear yet, but things have gotten progressively better. Thank you for your continuing thoughts, prayers, love and support.

I will let you know more when I know more.

Thank you.

November 21, 2014.

Well, the plan is to move her today and the insurance is behind the decision, again has little to do with reality, but an average timeline, oh and dollars. Does not matter, I'm spending $20K a year for this privilege!

Kathi is to move to the main Methodist, first for gall bladder evaluation; then heart evaluation by the cardiologist and cardio-thoracic surgeon, prior to proceeding with mitral valve replacement with porcine (pig) tissue. They want to do gall bladder removal too; seems kind of aggressive to me. I guess that's why I'm not a doctor.

Mitral Valve Surgery

Turns out, Kathi was moved to main Methodist tonight. Following the ambulance which was transporting her between facilities, that was basically a few blocks up the same street without lights and sirens, but apparently driver is used to going through red lights as he advanced in the middle of the intersection, while the oncoming traffic had left turn signal and there was a medical center police car in the lane next to the ambulance. During these times, you must insert humor, now and again. I could see the attendant in back with Kathi as he readjusted the equipment after they stopped on a dime. Kathi made it to the hospital safely.

First she was admitted to a room in Surgical Intensive Care Unit (SICU) and during the course of the night, she was moved to an isolation room in the same unit, because of her charts reflecting her MAC. Same thing happened when she was first diagnosed with MAC, the county center for disease control, wanted to quarantine our house, because they thought she had TB. She stayed in that 'corner room with a view' until her surgery. And the doctors got after it once she was set up in her room. The cardiologist performed the catheterization, inserting a number of sensors directly into her heart. From that point on, Kathi had to lay flat on her back and was not allowed to move her right leg. The sensors and telemetry monitor were tracking a number of heart rate and internal blood pressure readings.

November 22, 2014

Doctors ran an operational check on Kathi's gall bladder with dye. It works fine, so the gall bladder does not come out. Hallelujah!

November 23, 2014

Here we are completing the second full day at another hospital. It is a good thing. They've already removed the gall bladder tube, which was inserted on September 25 and not the gall bladder. The purpose of being here at the hospital is to replace the heart mitral valve, because Kathi had reached a plateau at the LTAC. She was not going to get any better and in all likelihood would definitely begin to get worse. The leaking heart was continuing to generate fluid to the lungs and Kathi could only be on CPAP for no more than 12 hours. She was starting to make good progress on physical therapy, by walking short distances, sitting up for long periods of time and doing some minimal arm exercises.

However, Kathi did not have a good night last night; after the contrast dye test on her gall bladder giving her nausea and being anxious all night long. Plus, part of her issues last night was not receiving all the right meds at the LTAC. So when they started giving them to her here, it created a change in her physiology. She has slept most of the day, received 2 Anointing of the Sick and 2 Spiritual Communion/ Blessings. Father F, whose ministry is the hospital and his parish are the patients, provided Anointing of the Sick as did Father D, a long-time friend. The first Spiritual Communion was also provided by Fr. F and the second by an evangelical Hebraic Christian, you know we've got to have those labels and titles. And Kathi was serenaded with two beautiful hymns sung by an angel. I woke up in the middle of the night speaking in tongues.

So, replacing the heart mitral valve should provide a dramatic improvement in Kathi's health.

Eulogy

November 24, 2014.

Last night, Kathi went into v-tach again, but was able to come out of it by coughing at the instructions of the attendees/nurses. During my morning prayers this morning, God told me to write Kathi's eulogy, see Figure 20141124-1. I wrote three pages, then ran out of writing, but made note to continue later with talking about our blessed grandchildren and what they mean to Kathi.

I go to visit Kathi, determined to find out when the heart surgery is going to be scheduled. Of course, I'm at the mercy of the doctors, not the other way around. I did notice upon my arrival that Kathi looked worse, however seemed to be sleeping peacefully, so I told the nurse I would be in the waiting room, in the event the doctors came by. I went into the waiting room and continued writing the eulogy about our grandchildren. I wrote what I could.

A couple hours later, I went back in to check on her and she was awake, I waited on her as best as I could and realized yesterday that she would not be going back to the LTAC to wean off the ventilator; her next facility will be in hospice. That was brought home later this evening when the cardiologist showed up.

Before I go there, I want to add yet another anecdote that is the circus called the healthcare industry. When Kathi was admitted to the Short-term Cardic Care hospital end of July/early August for her low BP, passing/blacking out/fainting and falling down; I had mentioned, maybe it's her arachnoid cyst – so they did a cranial CT scan which was reviewed by a neurologist in the hospital. Upon Kathi's discharge one of her follow-up instructions was to see a neurologist. Course we had to wait a few weeks for the referral process to take effect and that was due to Kathi's PCP's staff associating a wrong policy number with our name. No one called me, I had to initiate the call. The first call was to my insurance company to see if they had a referral on record to visit the neurologist, which they did not. My second call was to the PCP's staff and I mean staff, I spoke to 3 different people due to their specialization within the office. At any rate, it was 'B' who told me the insurance did not approve and began reading 'my' policy number back to me, until I asked her whose policy number is that? Once we got that squared away, the referral and subsequent appointment was accomplished within the same day. We go to the neurologist appointment and he tells us after showing us the first CT Scan taken several years ago, before Kathi's sinus surgery which discovered (the accidental cyst) and the one recently done in the hospital in August – no change in growth; the cyst is not your problem. That is good news of course, with baited breath. He then wants Kathi to visit 'internal' Ear, Nose, Throat specialists who focus on inner ear balance problems/issues. On our way from the appointment, we stop and talk to 'C', his staff person responsible for generating and tracking referrals. She told us to give her a couple of weeks and check back with her. A couple of weeks later, Kathi had already been in the hospital for a week.

Fast forward to today at 4:25 PM and Kathi's phone rings and someone leaves a voicemail. I listen to it and it's Carmen telling us the referral had been approved and forwarded onto the ENT specialists, we can go ahead and schedule appointment now. Incredible! If it had been a neuro problem, Kathi would be dead now, 2 months later and this has nothing to do with the Affordable Care Act. I called Carmen back and told all that had occurred since our visit to her office and to cancel the referral.

The Cardiologist shows up about 8:00 PM as is his modus-ope-randi and nurse 'B' retrieves me out of the waiting room. The doctor says now they are monitoring her elevated white cell counts and fever spikes from the gall bladder tube insertion area. But, as he continues to talk looking at Kathi's telemetry monitor and adjusting knobs on the cathertization tubes/sensors inserted in Kathi's heart last Friday night; he begins saying something else – the pressures in her heart are not right for surgery. That is why God told me to write Kathi's eulogy this morning. She is not going to have the required mitral valve sur-gery – now I wait for the doctors to tell me that. The cardiologist did tell me the A-Team doctors and surgeons are on call and waiting for the cardio-vascular (CV) surgery to be scheduled. I think he was just placating me in saying that.

November 24, 2014

Where do I start?

Let us begin by saying that each of us has a covenant with God. That covenant is our soul, our life which is a Gift. Kathi used her gift to bring the Love of Jesus to those who met her. Sometimes, there were those who did not understand her. Sometimes, I did not understand her. What she was giving, people did not want to accept. What Kathi was giving meant others would also have to give, their hearts were not necessarily ready for that unconditional commitment. In Kathi's larger than life heart, when others would reject that love, that gift of herself, she would be hurt and not understand how anyone could reject Love. I am just as guilty as the next person, yet I have been blessed that she saw something in me and stuck with me. She was saving my soul.

Kathi's favorite passage is from the first letter of St. Paul to the Corinthians, chapter 13 - insert - And she brought that home to me when we first met and "I" was searching into the cosmic unknown. She would tell me you do not need any of that crap!, It's Love, that's all there is and all you need. I can truthfully say she was not borrowing from the Beatles' song. She believed it with all her being.

At the same time, yes this saint was very human, no different than God's Holy Ones throughout human history. She cried when hurt, she got angry over that hurt, she would break things to release that anger. She was quick to anger, but just as quick at venting it. Most times she would get mad at me for not expressing anger at some event. We were as opposite as two people could get, she had all our common denominator was love. She had all of it and willing to share it. I had none of it and she was happy, but frustrated as she was continually filling that black hole in my heart. I'm sure she has shared that frustration with some of you here today.

Could she talk? Are you kidding me? That was one of the first things which attracted me to her (other then her natural beauty). I was star struck, incredulous! Why, how does she do that? She says what she is thinking! what a novel concept. Kathie did not have much of a filter, did not need one. This put alot, did I say alot? of people off. Then later in life, my mistake, I began schussling her, attempting to squelch that beauty we all know and love as Kathie. Was I successful? Yeah, right, for my

Grandchildren
children

we both agreed we
were not going to
a resort.

efforts, I would get to replace ~~something~~ inanimate
objects / household items.

She was so very excited to go on our recent trip to
Hawaii. She planned it, the whole thing, I partially
forced her into it. I put the onus on her, she
was a stay at home Gaba and I was working.
She was having a hard time finding something to
occupy her time, so I thought this would be
good for her. Reluctantly, at first, she dove right
into it, as she always does when accepting a
project, (a project like me). Unfortunately, I realize
now, it was all she could do to focus on staying
alive. And I was anxious about the trip to Hawaii
and how she would do, but we spent the money;
she actually did better than I anticipated. Her
health did control what we did, however we
did not mind as we were able to relax in paradise.
And we became short time celebrities in the
little town of Honokaa; watching the last two games
of the Finals at a place called the Landing.

Figure 20141124-1. Kathi's Eulogy.

Eulogy Addendum

She loves her grandchildren, when our first one was born, Kathi was already planning her retirement and all that she would do with Trinity. Her retirement occurred a little earlier as she retired to care for ill mother. Then along came Destiny, Lorelei, then Jovan, then Ewan, then …..

Kathi became a soccer grandmom, she made every effort to be at each grandchildren's special moments and events at school, dance class and drama class. She became familiar with most of their doctors and ensured Kathi knew who their dentist was so she could tell them how to treat her grandchildren.

She taught each of them to swim in both of our backyards, including our pseudo-grandchildren (niece and nephew); Molly and Collin. Jovan and Ewan will miss that attention, because pawpaw does not know how to swim.

At home, our grandchildren were the talk around our dinner table or tv trays, if you will. Kathi would tell me all about the day's events, whether it was a special shopping trip to Justus for the 'girls' or Mama K bringing the boys over for a visit in the daytime.

Where do I start? How does this end? This has not been easy. The last year has been a personal hell, not for me, but for Kathi. This exuberant, vivacious, and bigger than life woman had become a shell of the person. As a sidebar, Kathi's BFF, a massage therapist and an energist was massaging Kathi's feet today and felt no energy from Kathi. She had a bad gut feeling about the surgery.

November 25, 2014.

I finally spoke to the cardio-thoracic surgeon about an hour ago. The heart mitral valve replacement surgery is scheduled for 12:30 P.M. tomorrow. Otherwise, it'll be sometime next week. Be advised that Kathi faces many risks with this surgery. However, if she does not have the surgery, she will face the same risk(s) with no chance of recovery. The doctor/team will be here about 11 tomorrow a.m. to begin prepping. Tell everyone to pray for a successful surgery and rapid recovery for Kathi. Know once that hurdle has been overcome, she still faces weaning from the ventilator. I have gotten a room across the street at the motel 6 for the next 2 nights. PRAY!

November 26, 2014

This was going to be a big day for Kathi, getting the mitral valve replacement. She was scheduled for 12:30. At 11:20, one of the cardiologists came in her room looked directly at me and said "I guess you heard"? I said "heard what"? "There is an emergency cardiac patient who has pre-empted your surgery." Looks like we will have to wait until Friday. We do not want to begin your surgery at 7:00 PM. Ok. Kathi was very disappointed as was I. I went across the street, packed my bags and cancelled my second night at the hotel across the street from the hospital. I let the hotel know that I would probably be getting a room for two nights beginning tomorrow night, but had to wait for a firm surgery schedule.

3:56 PM.

Sorry it took so long to get this out, but Kathi's surgery was postponed. She was pre-empted by another 'emergency' surgery. The cardio-thoracic surgeon was performing another surgery at Stone Oak. Perhaps it was Divine Intervention; Kathi may not have been ready yet. We are waiting for the surgeon to come by and talk to us sometime after he's out of procedures at 6:00 PM, then we will know what time this Friday the surgery will occur. Please continue to pray.

The surgeon came by about 6:40 PM, first to apologize and also to tell us he did not want to begin a surgery of this magnitude at this late hour after having been in surgery all day. We agreed with that. He tells us the earliest he will be able to get to Kathi is 8:00 A.M. Monday morning. Kathi is vehemently shaking her head no. He then tells us about another surgeon, who is available to perform the surgery on Friday. The cardiologist had already briefed us earlier in the day about him, a brilliant surgeon who trained under the doctor who invented and innovated the heart transplant procedure in Houston and this surgeon was the first to accomplish heart transplants in San Antonio. Kathi wanted to get this done, no offense doctor, but I'm tired of waiting. So it was set, now we wait for the schedule.

November 27, 2014 (Thanksgiving)

Today was a day of rest for my wife. Kathi and the nurses fought most of the previous night trying to keep her blood pressure up. She was wore out and her body needed the rest. There was a Divine intervention which occurred yesterday, she was not ready for the surgery.

We found out today that surgery is scheduled for tomorrow morning at 8:00 A.M. and the team will begin prepping her about 7:30. Hallelujah! I called the hotel and reserved a room for the next two nights. My bag with three days' worth of lounge clothes was already packed and in my truck.

Kathi has her last meal at supper, a traditional Thanksgiving Turkey dinner. Kathi barely touched her food as has been the case over the last nine months. A few bites of turkey, mashed potatoes and pumpkin pudding with whipped cream, was all she could muster. She picks at it, total of 7 bites, mostly the pumpkin pudding with whip cream on top. The doctors told us that the procedures would take approximately five hours and that Kathi's recovery would take just as long. That is why I reserved two nights.

Fortunately, my son and his wife live close by the hospital and my son brought us a care package of thanksgiving dinners in two plates. I gobbled up one of the plates my son brought in the SICU waiting room while Kathi slept. Later that evening, I put the second plate in the hotel room refrigerator; I had also packed a few beers.

Surgery

November 28, 2014

I arrived at Kathi's room at 6:00 A.M., I did not want to be late. Her room was dark and Kathi was sleeping peacefully. I kept it that way and stood by the window praying. I began the Liturgy of the hours facing East and then about 20 minutes later, Kathi's youngest aunt showed up. Her aunt prayed over Kathi in her inimitable way and woke her up, realizing her error backed away, since Kathi was awake, I let her know I was there. Then she faded off again. The nurse K, told us the team would actually show up closer to 8:00. But, you could sense the SICU staff prepping about 7:15 A.M. The Cardio-Vascular Operating Room (CVOR) nurse, also named K came in about 7:50, told us what was going to happen and about five minutes later, the rest of the team, an anesthesiologist and another nurse came in but had to wait for one more nurse, as Kathi's transfer required a few hands to manage all the equipment. K informs us the doctor would start the procedure by having to carefully cut through the scar tissue, which carries with it a significant risk of bleeding. As a precaution, they gave Kathi a transfusion of 2 pints of blood on Thanksgiving.

Then after performing the mitral valve replacement, they would perform the cryo-maze procedure. The mitral valve would take about 3 hours and the cryo-maze about 90 minutes. Kelly tells us we're ready to roll and we walk with her to the operating room elevators and she puts key in and opens doors and we wait for Kathi and her entourage.

Apparently, she is overridden from some other floor and the doors close. In the meantime, K goes to check on the delay with Kathi. She comes back reopens elevator doors and about that time, Kathi and her tour come into view around the corner. We all get on the elevator and go down to the 5th floor. We follow the gurney and Kelly shows us the doors to the operating room and then takes us to the Neuro Cardio Vascular (NCV) surgical waiting room. She tells us that prepping Kathi will take about 45 minutes and that operation will begin taking place in earnest at around 9:00 A.M.. Meanwhile, she will keep me apprised of status/progress via hourly phone call updates. Kathi's aunt, who is only 3 years older than Kathi, was with me in the NCV waiting room. Once we got there and picked our places, I went downstairs to get some breakfast from the cafeteria; it was a big burrito with everything in it. Her aunt had brought her own food; yes I offered to get her something. I got back before 9 and started working on my caregiver book; then we started talking about religion, I did not work on my book anymore that day. She began giving me insight into her faith, her conversations with and missions from God, her several missionary trips to the Holy Land and the Scriptural basis for those missions. She tells me that she prays before 'accepting' the missions from God and I tell her, like my confirmation namesake; St. Peter, I usually do not question and that early in my formation, someone had told me He only knocks once. I realize now, that was incorrect or perhaps I interpreted incorrectly. Kathi's aunt and I had a wonderful faith sharing experience, we are not that far apart. Plus, she was a former CCD teacher and we all know there are more former Catholics then current ones. We must be better teachers about the Scriptural basis of our traditions.

About 10:45, the CVOR nurse K calls me and said they just finished the cryomaze procedure and that the surgeon was starting to size the tissue for the mitral valve. She apologized for not having called sooner, but she had to monitor the heart/lung machine. Kathi's aunt Dottie said a beautiful prayer of thanks. At 12:15, K called again and they were starting the mitral valve replacement. Aunt Dottie said another prayer of thanks, calling on Kathi's guardian angels to protect her in the operating room. When she prayed this, I envisioned the guardian angels surrounding/encircling Kathi on the operating table at an elevated level; with doctors, nurses and the equipment of the OR in view. When I shared this vision with aunt Dottie after her prayer, she said that is exactly what she saw. About 15 minutes later, aunt Dottie excused herself to use the restroom and confided in me later, she had gone to the doors of the OR and prayed over them.

At 1:10 PM, the CVOR nurse K called me and told me they were done 'buttoning' up Kathi and she would probably be back in her room about 1:30 and the Dr. would visit with us in the SICU waiting room at the same time. Kelly mentioned the only concern now was whether Kathi's heart would wake up on its own.

Like clockwork, nurse K came into the waiting room first, said everything went smoothly, even though they had prepared for every eventuality, the surgery was uneventful. The surgeon came in right after nurse K , said the surgery went well, Kathi did well and is stable.

Praise the LORD, for he is good;

sing praise to our God, for he is gracious;

it is fitting to praise him.

The LORD rebuilds Jerusalem;

the dispersed of Israel he gathers.

He heals the brokenhearted

and binds up their wounds.

He tells the number of the stars;

he calls each by name.

Great is our Lord and mighty in power;

to his wisdom there is no limit.

The LORD sustains the lowly;

the wicked he casts to the ground.[21]

And this was email our son sent out to our family and friends prayer distribution list:

Ok, just to drop everyone a quick note, my mom just went into surgery to replace the mitrial valve in her heart. It will take at least 5-6 hours, but possibly longer depending on how she reacts to everything. Please keep her in your thoughts and prayers.

Thank you.

The ICU nurse called the waiting room about 2:30 asking me how many members were in the waiting room, I told her six and she said for us to come into Kathi's room. I asked her, is Kathi awake already and she told me no, she just did not want to have to repeat our instructions relative to visitors. So, I grabbed everyone and we proceeded to Kathi's room and the nurse told us; no more than 2 visitors at a time, limited to 15 minutes. Then we went back out to the waiting room, as other family members came by to visit Kathi. True to what Kelly had told us earlier this morning, she said Kathi's recovery would take as long, if not longer than the actual procedures. Kathi was still asleep at 7:45 PM, when I returned to the hotel and ate my second thanksgiving plate, which I chased with a beer.

November 29, 2014.

I slept in this morning, ate one of the bananas and grapefruit I had packed for breakfast, packed up everything and put it in my truck, then checked out of the hotel, leaving my truck in their parking lot. It was a cold morning, I believe it got down to freezing, we're not used to that in San Antonio, even in the winter, but the sun was out, so it was going to warm up. I went to check on Kathi for a couple of hours; she was still in and out. I let her know, I was going home to wash clothes and check on the house and I would be back later. She already seems stronger. I love you. Praise God!

I returned around 5:30 PM, Kathi is still groggy and asking what happened? I start at the beginning and bring her up to date. I go into the waiting room at 6:30 for the report/shift change and return at 8:00 to meet her night crew and 'make sure' everything is running smoothly. I then go home for the night.

Recovery

November 30, 2014. First Sunday of Advent.

I served at two Masses this morning, went home, ate breakfast, changed clothes, made some more food for the honeybirds and washed/ dried a load of clothes.

Oh, ye of <u>LITTLE</u> FAITH! I'm stuck in mud. I'm paralyzed; I know this must be some kind of depression side effect. Even with the good news of a successful surgery on Friday, I'm mired down in myopia of pity party. I got to the hospital today about 5:43 PM. Kathi is a little more aware/awake and agitated. She is still a little confused by all that has happened, thus far. Today at 6:28 her heart sinus rhythm was just doing some spikes and dipped to 39 and 40. I mentioned this to nurse and she said not to worry, it's been jumping all over the place and doctor is aware of it and he's not worried. I guess as long as it does not go down to zero (0). Right before I left for shift change, Kathi wanted to write something, so I got the clipboard, which was probably a mistake on my part; I could not read what she wrote and while she was writing, her HR jumped to over 100 and her systole BP dropped below

80; both set off monitor alarm. I apologized to the nurse and she said no problem.

So it was time to go out and let them prepare for shift change at 6:30. They put in a NG tube again, because her belly is distended and she is not passing gas. No food except through the tube, only ice chips by mouth.

Her involuntary familial tremors have returned; and it's in her feet now too. The doctor did say it might take a few days for her heart to get into rhythm and I probably should not watch the monitor.

I came back after shift change at 8:00 PM, Kathi was grimacing in pain, I captured night nurse who told me she was getting pain meds. Again I'm watching monitor and I notice some alarm info at bottom RH corner of the telemetry monitor –

- HR Lo – 0 – 19:43
- Systole LO – 41 19:43

And up in the HR monitor range there was red flag showing No Paper, so I'm hanging around to make sure Kathi gets attention. Nurse gives Kathi pain meds and goes to her patient next door. I'm talking to Kathi about inane things (Christmas presents for boys, vacuum cleaner for condo) and her HR begins fluctuating dropping into the 40s, then hits 26 which sets off alarm and BP drops as well into alarm range. Both then stabilize and the annotation reflects in lower right hand corner box (alarm) – along with previous alarm readings, and still No Paper.

- HR LO – 26 – 20:24

I went home about 10:30, once I was comfortable that Kathi was comfortable and resting peacefully.

December 1, 2014.

I'm not happy sharing Kathi with everyone else. Today, she went into V-Tach several times and the only thing the staff did was come in and silence the alarms. Course, at one time the entire staff was in another room for a 'coded' patient, I went out of Kathi's room to find out where everyone was and I saw them spilling out of a room like it was some sort of training session as one nurse was applying CPR. Someone in the crowd of 'orientees' saw me, came and closed the double doors; which separated the sections. The alarm for that 'code' had been going off for quite awhile.

December 2, 2014.

I let Kathi's BFF go in and visit, while I hung out in the waiting room with Kathi's brother. Her BFF came out later and told me that a case manager was in Kathi's room asking 'basic' questions. I blew up and asked who the person was and what did he look like? I went looking for him, found him and I let him know in no uncertain terms, he would not involve anyone else but me when it came to Kathi's 'case' and care. He was using excuse that Kathi appeared lucid and said it was okay. I asked him why her friend was answering your questions. I also told him that Kathi is pretty much in a dream state, thinks you're a dream and will not remember it tomorrow.

Then on night shift, nurse told me that Kathi's bowels/intestines are blocked and gave a name; Ileus (paralytic), which may require surgery to relieve. That is why they're continuing to move her around and going to attempt to sit her up.

December 4, 2014.

As y'all prayer warriors may have already heard; Kathi's heart surgery to replace the weak mitral valve was a success last Friday. They also performed a cryomaze (internal ablation – to attempt to fix the afib; little does Dr. Sean know), while they had the heart open, before actually replacing the mitral valve. Some of the risks which they made me aware of during the phone updates while she was in surgery, was there was the potential for severe bleeding while the doctor was cutting through the scar tissue already there, a delicate procedure. They pushed ahead with the surgery, because Kathi had progressed as far as she was going to, considering her inability to wean completely off the ventilator because her bad mitral valve was leaking fluid back into her lungs. It was a continuous cycle or the medical term is congestive heart failure.

All of these procedures occurred during the 5 hour operation; they took her into the OR at 8:15 A.M. and she was back in her room at 13:30 PM. The CVOR nurse came into the waiting room told me the entire surgery went by the book and, she said they were prepared for anything and everything based on Kathi's health history and condition, but essentially was 'uneventful'; aunt D said Praise God and I said Hallelujah. The surgeon then came and told me pretty much the same thing, he was very humble. I believe I caught a glimpse of 'why' Kathi's surgery was postponed on Wednesday.

So, since Saturday various tubes and sensors have been removed from Kathi, her HR remains 70-72 range, pulse ox 96-100, except when she bends her finger, and BP is high for her. No fever, no infections. They continue to wean her during the day from the ventilator (she's on CPAP during the day).

A couple of days ago, the ID doctor came by and let us know that the infection had completely destroyed the mitral valve.

All the above leads to this:

Doctor came in a couple hours ago:

1. They're going to start 'feeding' her today
2. They're going to continue to wean her off the ventilator
3. Tomorrow they may try completely to take her off the ventilator and put the speaking cap on the trach

They're looking at moving her 'down' (out of ICU) in a couple of days (when the doctor said this, besides the sudden catch in my throat, I think the ac filters in her room must've been broke and I think they are here in the waiting room as I write this).

Thank you Jesus! Keep praying!

December 7, 2014.

Kathi seems to be progressing except for her weaning off the ventilator and a BM. It's been over a week and she has yet to have a BM. Earlier today, the cardiologist was talking to the nurses about moving Kathi back to the LTAC. When I got here today, her ventilator tube was full of blood at the trach and the tube itself. Apparently, there was a plan to replace it, because she was sleeping and there was a replacement kit laying on her belly, still unopened. I brought it to the attention of the Respiratory Therapist (RT), who it seems was not the one who put it there, since he was fixing to depart the room and go get one. (Coordination? Anybody actually read the charts? Anyone making entries on the charts?)

Kathi woke up and the thought of having to move back to LTAC got her spooled up for the day and she began coughing. The RT person revised some settings on the ventilator, which only made it worse and at the same time, decided to finally change and clean out Kathi's ventilator tube/trach. Lo and behold; there was a blood plug on the end of the tube which went down her throat. Seems to me, the suction with the younker would catch that obstruction. At any rate, she really began to freak out because she was not on the machine while he was cleaning the equipment; she was on straight oxygen mode, but the damage had already been started. She had been on CPAP all day, but now at 3:00 PM, he put her back on the respirator, even though Kathi had told the pulmonologist earlier today, she does better on CPAP! So, she began asking for Xanax and pain meds, her regular nurse was assisting to transport the patient next door to floor downstairs. It was not quick enough, so I punched the nurse button for Kathi. Another nurse came and began taking care of her med needs. Her regular nurse got back and thanked the other nurse. I told Kathi I was going to give her a break and go in the waiting room for a while and call the priest and tell him I was not going to be able to serve at the 5:30 Mass, because Kathi is having a bad day. I could not leave her. I guess that answers my question and probably because her body/psyche has been trained that way for so long. One good or 'up' day, then 2-3 days to recover.

She had a bad fit of coughing and not able to catch her breath. The heart surgery has had some beneficial impact and effect. She cannot stay at the LTAC forever! And the last 2 days which she reminded me of, I did not pray over or bless her. I told her that I had recognized those omissions myself (at home later in the evening). Is this a homily of some sort during Advent?

And this waiting room is a big distraction of humanity. I guess families are just venting nervous energy.

Where do I start this chapter? Do I begin with describing our idyllic lives to reflect normalcy and how illness interrupts all aspects and elements of your lives; that of the patient (of course), the caregiver, family and friends? The longer the illness, the more you recognize family and friends and it boils down to you the caregiver – to stand by the patient;

your loved one. Because everyone else except a few have gone back to their daily lives. This should be a quick dose of reality, life goes on. What? The world does not revolve around me? You and the patient are left alone to face the challenges and decisions of the doctors and insurance company on your own. This is where the mettle of the caregiver's intestinal fortitude becomes seriously tested.

And how often the caregiver gets frustrated, runs out of gas, gets exasperated with the patient, the system, loses patience, and takes on guilt for feeling the patient is overreacting. No, we do not know how it feels, we cannot even imagine the pain (I've never had my chest cracked open, Kathi has had it done twice now), the fear, the anxiety or lack of success the patient is feeling. Our chest is not the one split down the middle or we're not the one who cannot breathe because we have MAC, pseudomonas, Bronchiectasis. For this patient, that is what it boils down to; she cannot breathe!

December 9, 2014.

Kathi is still in SICU. However, yesterday, she was completely off the ventilator breathing on her own. The RT person said they would put her on CPAP from 11:00 PM to 7:00 A.M. this morning while she slept. She is still a little anxious about being away from the ventilator, since she had that episode at the LTAC a few weeks ago. Her anxieties are rising, because rumors abounded yesterday about her being moved back to the LTAC to finish the weaning process. Hopefully, I can get the doctors to agree on where she is actually going to go and when. I actually got to see her walk in her room yesterday and she had 3 positive events she/the doctors/nurses have been waiting for, since surgery. She is still being fed total parenteral nutrition (TPN), but that should change shortly (again Dr. Sean speaking). She had the NG tube put back in through her nose, because some of her systems took awhile 'to wake up' after surgery.

I just spoke to the nurse and Case Manager, they told me Kathi slept through the night breathing on her own!!! I am going to have to replace the ac filters here before she gets home. Oh wait, the heater/ac isn't turned on.

Physical Therapy is fixing to come in and do some more exercises. And it sounds like she will be moving back to LTAC today if they have a bed, to finish the rehab process; breathing, speaking, learning to walk again, and eating. The case manager was facilitating that when I called. Praise God! Hallelujah!

December 10, 2014.

Kathi is off the ventilator and has been since Monday morning. In fact the RT person made a production of moving the ventilator out of Kathi's room yesterday, throwing away the tubes, and disposable items. Kathi also walked around the SICU yesterday. Speech therapy came in and put on a speaking cap, so she can save her carpel tunnel from all the writing she's been doing in past weeks, and lower her frustration level, because none of us, including the nurses, doctors or speech therapist know how to read lips. Kathi had some applesauce, cran/grape juice and orange sherbert; part of swallow tests to see if she could start eating again. Finally, she will be moving back to the LTAC as soon as they have a bed available. It did not happen last night, may happen today.

LTACF

December 11, 2014.

Kathi arrived at the LTACF in room 108 last night. Her night nurse was being assisted by the CNA. As they were still getting Kathi situated, getting her into the system (Pixsys?), the nurse had to check on getting Kathi's requested pain meds; and had to place call to the Dr.? I asked two RT nurses for ice chips, but they had to check, I asked, wasn't that in transfer charts, maybe,–but the process is to check the system. However, her information has to be input first, I asked who does that and when, course wrong people to ask. Meanwhile, Kathi's nurse is MIA looking for pain meds and she is being paged on the PA for ICU. That is quite a lot of ground to cover between room 108 and ICU? I'm guessing LTAC must really be short-staffed tonight.

December 12, 2014. My sister's birthday.

Kathi's transfer back to the LTAC did occur on Wednesday evening. The Kathi that we all know and love continues to have positive, loving effect on those she meets, even without being able to speak and in her less than healthy condition. The nursing staff at Methodist medical center, gave her a farewell 'parade' as they came from all over to tell her goodbye, they love her and will miss her, some were crying, while making her promise to come back and visit them when she is well.

She actually received that call and Mission from Father Fausto on Tuesday when he came by to pray over and bless her; to come back and minister to the patients.

Yesterday morning, Kathi gets a kiss from her (male) pulmonologist who was very happy to see her improved condition from the last time he saw her before her heart surgery at Methodist. All the nurses and staff who saw her before at LTAC are making their way to her room to see her and visit with her. They are all excited about a good news story.

PT will exercise her in earnest beginning Monday; meanwhile, they left some one pound hand weights to practice reps with over the week-end. She got the swallow test again yesterday and passed. She is eating regular food or 'mechanical' soft food, she has what looks like beef-a-roni, carrots and corn, with a hearty, robust strawberry high calorie 'shake' right now.

The pulmonologist just came by (no kiss) and said he was going to change the trach and that he's thinking it will come off (I asked him completely? And he said yes) in a couple of days! Praise God!

Kathi is not in the ICU at LTAC, she is in the general hospital and visiting hours for the general hospital is 9:00 A.M. to 9:00 P.M. She has a private room with a view of the courtyard, and she has 3 chairs, or 2 if she happens to be sitting in her special recliner as she was most of the day today.

You are witness to the power and miracles wrought by your prayers; answered by God. Please continue to keep lifting Kathi up. Thank you!

Amen and Hallelujah!

December 13, 2014.

The pulmonologist came today and downsized the trach in Kathi's throat. It remains capped with a speaking cap and Kathi is thrilled to be able to talk. There was no PT or OT today, being Saturday. I served at the 5:30 PM Vigil Mass, brought Kathi communion and stayed until 9:00 PM.

December 14, 2014.

I served at the 7:30 A.M. and 9:00 A.M. Masses today, this third Sunday of Advent. I went home, changed clothes and ate some lunch. Then I spent the rest of the day tending to Kathi's needs.

December 15, 2014.

Today, the pulmonologist on rounds toward the end of the business day removed the trach altogether! Kathi had much trepidation as we kept trying to explain to her, she has not been using it for the last several days. I also used the ploy since she had been complaining about the collar holding it in place, that the collar too will be gone and not irritating your neck. The process itself occurred without much fanfare, took about twenty minutes and most of that time was spent in cleaning and covering the site and opening. The trach and adjoining tube was just pulled out.

Once it was done, Kathi was relieved and happy that this was an indication of positive progress toward recovery and recuperation. We prayed a prayer of thanksgiving.

December 16, 2014.

I spent a good portion of the day Christmas shopping for our grand-children on line. It's amazing. The retailers are pretty smart. They have developed a 'wish list' and my tech savvy grandchildren (or their par-ents) have listed all their material Christmas desires on this website. All I had to do was select the 'gifts', have them giftwrapped for a couple of extra dollars, sent to my house and place them under the four foot tall silver tree with blue ornaments. Since I ordered so much, I did not have to 'pay' for shipping. I put them all on tracking alerts for my email and cell phone, since the presents were coming from all over the globe. The promise was they would all be here by December 24th.

December 17, 2014.

Kathi has to remind me sometimes to pray over and bless her. I remembered today on my own before I left, but she told me something very profound. "I have a deacon in my house, I might as well use him; besides when you pray over and bless me, it comforts me".

We pray.

In the name of the Father, Son and Holy Spirit ✞.

Heavenly Father,

We give thanksgiving and praise for the miracles you have wrought thus far in Kathi, as she has provided witness to doctors, staff, nurses and well-wishers to the power of prayer. We come before you seeking continued healing for Kathi, we ask that you surround Kathi with your healing presence and that you send her guardian angels to protect and keep her safe. We ask for the Love of Jesus to ease Kathi's anxiety and calm her fears. We ask you to send your Holy Spirit to give Kathi strength, courage and perseverance to meet the challenges ahead in her recovery and healing. We ask for the Blessed Mother Mary to wrap Kathi in her loving arms and comfort her as only a mother can. These things we ask through Jesus your Son. Amen.

May almighty God Bless and heal you. In the name of the Father, Son and Holy Spirit. . . ✞. Amen.

December 18, 2014.

Kathi has done some extensive PT/OT today. She is sleeping good now and I'm sure they'll be waking her up with supper soon. I met with the PT team and case manager today. They're talking about removing another tube tomorrow and possibly on Tuesday or Wednesday next week; she will move to a rehab facility for a couple of weeks to work on physical reconditioning. Got the list of rehab places, probably going to stay local to this facility. The Physical Medicine and Rehabilitation (PM&R) resident who comes here works out of this other rehab place 2 blocks away; it's the frontrunner, I know where all the local restaurants are now, but I've got some tours to do. I'll call and make some tour appointments to check the places out tomorrow. The potential for her to be home before my birthday. It is just beginning to seem surreal. When she does come home there will still be need for some home health care and some special equipment around the house, but to have her home!!!! Prayer of thanksgiving every day. Glory to God in the Highest.

Praise God! Amen! Hallelujah!

December 19, 2014.

Kathi took her first shower in over three months today! She asked her OT attendant if she could just take a nap on the bench in the shower with the water pouring over her. Baptism, a new birth, a re-birth.

December 24, 2014.

Kathi was transferred to HealthSouth RIOSA room # 504 at 9119 Cinnamon Hill, yesterday. The place is basically 3 left turns from the parking lot of the LTAC. Left turn out of the LTAC parking lot onto Floyd Curl, left turn on Hamilton Wolfe, left turn onto Cinnamon Hill – oh I forgot, the fourth left turn is into HealthSouth RIOSA parking lot. Before she left LTAC, they removed the pic lines in her left arm yesterday. Please continue to pray for her strength and physical reconditioning. Merry Christmas!

I served as deacon at the 3:00 PM vigil Mass and midnight Mass. I served as deacon of the Altar and my brother Deacon served as Deacon of the Word and he proclaimed the Gospel in chant at the midnight Mass. What a beautiful service. It was standing room only, all ages.

December 25, 2014.

First I would like to begin with a little medical information from this link: http://www.medicinenet.com/bronchitis_acute/article.htm
Bronchitis describes a group of symptoms (including airway inflammation, over-production of mucous, and cough), which can have various causes:

- *If the cause of the bronchitis is viral or bacterial,* ***it can be contagious****.*

- *If the cause of the bronchitis is due to smoking, air pollution, or other inhaled irritants,* ***it is not contagious****.*

The purpose of this public service announcement is due to a relative visiting Kathi yesterday with 'non' contagious bronchitis. Their names are omitted to protect the arrogant, selfish and stupid. If you think you are sick; do not visit Kathi. In fact, you can be putting the entire hospital patients at risk with their diminished immune systems, if you're sick, by entering the hospital; that is of course, unless you're being admitted. I'm a little miffed at your laisse faire attitude toward my wife's life.

Kathi spent Christmas with her son/daughter-in-law and four of her five grandchildren. Her BFF visited her for a couple of hours and her brother and sister-in-law also visited, bringing a Christmas arrangement. Kathi's spirits were buoyed by the visitors and being able to see, hug and talk to her grandchildren for the first time in over 3 months.

Kathi was helped (more like observed) to her walker from her bed by the tech/cna and she walked without assistance to/from the restroom and without the oxygen tank. When she got back she was panting and put the cannula back on as she was supposed to do. You should have seen her, bound and determined, moving faster than I've seen her in quite some time and I told her that too. Praise God!

Later in the evening, I got to help her stand-up from her bed, while she was standing, I got me a hug from a tall good-looking blonde, then I straightened out her bed and tucked her in. Thank you, Lord. In the last vitals before I left her BP was low, so they did not administer the replacement anti-arrhythmia medicine, although her HR was 79 (so that is good).

Please continue to pray for her.

I pray your Christmas was joyous and spent with your loved ones, if not present, then in your heart and your Christmas season will continue to be joyous, loving and heartfelt. God Bless You.

December 26, 2014.

I spent Christmas 2014 with Kathi at the hospital, actually physical rehabilitation facility. I spent the morning in sorrowful reflection (pity party?). During the shift change, the daytime charge nurse was making turnover rounds with nightshift nurse; 'Cate'. She began by introducing Kathi with 'pericarditis'; I immediately informed them, that was over 40 years ago and Kathi corrected them by saying 'endocarditis. And it seemed they ignored what we were telling them, I guess because we're civilians and do not know what we're talking about. I wonder what other inaccuracies are in Kathi's charts. Something, I will query today when I provide them with a medical power of attorney (MPOA).

I want to spend this morning reviewing my diary for this past year as it may be relative to caregiving, because Kathi's ordeal did not just begin on September 23, 2014.

And now more from the continuing saga known as the healthcare industry. Kathi received a call today from her 'former' cardiologist's office, the voicemail and subsequent call back were telling Kathi that her echocardiogram and cardiologist office visit were being cancelled, because the insurance had not approved them. These appointments had been made on August 14 from her Infectious Disease physician. Good thing she was in the hospital!

It may be in the insurance company's infinite wisdom, they figured out Kathi was in the hospital and did not 'need' these appointments. However, I do not know, because I have not been kept apprised through my insurance company of claims, referrals or rejections through any Explanation of Benefits statements. My Insurance provider account on line shows $0 relative to claims for the year of 2014. I have not been able to access my files, reason I've been checking periodically, is so I'm not 'surprised' when the bills start rolling in.

December 30, 2014.

Kathi has been undergoing about 6 hours a day of therapy from 8:00 a.m. until 4:00 p.m. They are still struggling with her BP (too low), which means they are unable to give her the anti-arrhythmia medicine for her heart. This morning she's not feeling too hot. Please continue to pray for her healing and recovery.

If you will allow me, I would like to ask for some additional prayers.

Dear Prayer Warriors,

My family continues to receive miracles from your prayers. I want to thank you. I also want to give you example of how quickly prayers are answered.

Many of you have prayed more than once for our grand-daughter (nieta); Trinity. When I went to visit Kathi yesterday afternoon, there she was visiting Kathi (GaGa) with her daddy. Mike had just taken Trinity to a follow-up appointment for her broken left arm/shoulder, which occurred on September 12 and the doctor said they would prob-ably be removing the rods in her arm bones sometime next month. From Kathi's visit, they were then going out to Castroville, so her daddy could have the doctor look at his hand that he injured in a work accident. Castroville was the nearest medical center to his work site where he injured his hand a couple of weeks ago and it started bothering/hurting him the night before. As they were leaving, about 5:45 PM, I had an ominous/bad feeling–this is where you should recognize an opportunity to act. Instead, I told them I loved them and to be careful.

Every evening before I leave Kathi, visiting hours end at 8:00 PM, I pray over Kathi and bless her. Last night, I added the prayer that "God protect Trinity and send her guardian angels to keep her safe". Not too long or wordy.

About 11:00 PM last night, I got a frantic call from my daughter, whom you've also prayed for many times. She is physically disabled and legally blind from the Lupus steroids side effects. Trinity and her daddy had been in an accident, a serious one. Her daddy was driving on the way home and come over a rise on Loop 410 near Marbach road and there was an abandoned vehicle parked in the fast lane. He tried to avoid it, clipped it and his truck flipped, skidding on the top for about a hundred yards. Trinity was in her seat belt in the back seat of the crew cab. Her daddy was not wearing his seat belt. The front passenger window on the crew cab busted out and Trinity told her mama all she could see was sparks and gravel flying by, as she was hanging suspended from the seatbelt and that she could not see her daddy. Trinity is relatively unharmed other than the trauma and bruises from the shoulder harness. She also told her mama that all their stuff was all over the road.

Two of Trinity and her daddy's guardian angels were following directly behind them. One of them was a registered nurse. The nurse and her friend rendered aid providing a blanket for her daddy and an HEB sweater from the nurse's friend for Trinity. They called 911 and stayed with them until EMS arrived and they provided witness to the police. He was not swerving or speeding. They have kept Trinity overnight for observation at University Hospital in room #149 (7th floor) and they have her in a neck brace. Her daddy was also saved by this miracle, with some stitches on his face and his lip. Praise God!

Trinity was released from the hospital this afternoon, I know, I went to pick up Trinity and our daughter to take them home, since I was practically around the corner with Kathi. Her daddy had gone with a friend to the impound lot to retrieve/salvage personal belongings, work tools, equipment and contract files. Her daddy remembered nothing of the accident, except grabbing a hold of the steering wheel for his life and that his arms really hurt. Trinity remembered everything in calm clarity; this is her recount, as told to my daughter and me on the ride home from the hospital.

She was screaming so loud, she could not hear her screams anymore. Calming down and at peace when she felt the presence of her 'daddy'. Not closing her eyes, keeping her eyes on the broken window as the sparks and gravel flew by, knowing once they stopped skidding that was their way out! Then of course, she remembers shaking from side to side (shock) when the nurse and friend rendered aid.

This is amazing calmness for a ten year old. Nothing is impossible with God. Pray incessantly!

Please pray for Trinity's healing and rapid recovery and that the accident did not add any problems for her.

January 1, 2015.

It has been such a whirlwind, that I have not even reflected on what it has meant to serve in my first Advent and Christmas season as an ordained Deacon. Unfortunately, I'm thinking it is because I went through the rubrics, mechanics or motions of the celebrations. I was not present, instead focusing on the mechanics and complaining to the rectory about communication and coordination of which readings were going to be used for the six Christmas Eve vigil Masses versus the readings for the Midnight Mass. That is not a fair assessment, as I enjoyed serving the Lord and witnessing to His children in my small way, as I have been called.

After Kathi's heart surgery; it seemed the change began overnight and she began to improve. So, I was able to serve at all four Advent Sundays, the bi-lingual Mass for the Immaculate Conception, the bi-lingual Mass for Our Lady of Guadalupe, one Christmas Eve vigil Mass and the bi-lingual Midnight Mass. Somewhat of a blessing relative to the bi-lingual Masses, I have begun to read the intercessory prayers (of the faithful), half of which are in Spanish. This actually began with the Assumption Mass in August. It seems this is another call. My three years of taking Spanish in high school, albeit in the Midwest, where at the time, late 1960s, was in preparation for this, even though I did not have much call for practice. Then of course, moving here to San Antonio and working at Kelly AFB, I learned the local vernacular and spent probably the first ten years at Kelly 'correcting' the use of local Spanish versus the Castilian Spanish I had learned in school. I have yet to proclaim the Gospel in Spanish and that is what I must do before I can serve at the Spanish Mass, this is my emphasis. I'm thinking this is what I will use my last gift certificate for, which I received as gifts for my ordination.

I was blessed to be serving at the New Year 's Day Solemnity of Mary, Mother of God Mass, which did have an impact on me. And no, it was not enhanced by a previous evening's celebration. I was taking a shower at midnight, cleansing myself of the suffering of 2014. The Mass brought joy to me and perhaps a closer realization of who Mary is; the Ark of the (New) Covenant (Word). At the recession, I was telling every woman; "Happy Mother's Day!". This is a confession, I have never really been a Marianist, I've always had my focus on Jesus. I believe my heart is continuing to evolve in metanoia, as it should, which is a lifelong journey. Praise God! Open my heart, Lord!

Kathi has come a long way. Kathi sat in the chair while we visited. She is in the shower on her own. She walked, with the aid of a walker to the bathroom, got herself situated in the bathroom, turned on the water, washed and dried herself. She came back out on her own, I did help her get back into her bed, but I believe I may have been just a crutch. I helped her get back in bed; but I told her how impressed I was at the strides she has made in just a week, even compared to where she was this time last year as she slept most of our New Year's cruise in the gulf. She is gaining independence, day by day, all Glory and Praise to God Almighty! Amen!

January 2, 2015.

Happy New Year! Thank you for your continued prayers for Kathi and my family.

As coordination goes, current facility (RT) was attempting to wean her off oxygen, making her anxious, but more importantly not really knowing her pulmonary history/condition. They acquiesced once they called in a real pulmonologist who only had to look at her charts to assess whether to wean her or not. That would be a not and Kathi even mentioned last night; she has resigned herself to the potential for having to remain on oxygen when she comes home. She is still not out of the woods, the other day she was doing PT and asked the RT to take her pulse ox during a break. It was 78 with oxygen. It's supposed to be above 90. It was 84 the day EMS took her to ER on September 23. They are also still balancing her BP and heart meds. Her involuntary familial (essential) tremors have been more prominent since surgery and now involve her feet as well. However, one thing is certain, Kathi is bound and determined to do this even to the extent of walking a few steps unaided to grab her walker. I have to tell her to slow down and be careful. I am anxiously awaiting her return home, which is still a to be determined (TBD), from 'team' meeting on Tuesday. Another upside, she has been making daily requests to me for grooming/make-up products.

Please continue to pray for her.

The rehab facility took a chest x-ray this morning and they say Kathi has pneumonia. More later. Pray! Apologize for not getting back to you sooner. Kathi does not have pneumonia, course we had to wait for the long week-end before the rehab facility could obtain other chest x-rays for comparison. Kathi and I told them on Friday when the nurse told us the specific areas of indication; that the radiologist was looking at MAC scar tissue. The doctor had called for a chest x-ray, because Kathi was coughing a lot. Yes, she has bronchiectasis or did you not see that in the charts. After the x-ray, the radiologist made the call of pneumonia, not having any other x-rays for comparison, or awareness of patient's history, so much for objectivity. I told the nurse there were x-rays and CT scans of Kathi's lungs all over the state of Texas, that they can access for comparison sake.

Trinity and her daddy are recovering, although he is discovering new bumps, bruises and aches by the hour. His lips swelling has gone down, but he has gained a black eye and he is having trouble with his legs. They enjoyed New Year's Eve in their driveway with fireworks. They were supervised by her mama and a friend.

January 3, 2015

A new doctor (to the rehab facility) came by to check on Kathi, what specifically drove her visit is the rumor of pneumonia. I repeated to the doctor, what I told the nurse last night; there were x-rays and CT scans of Kathi's lungs all over the state of Texas, that they can access for comparison sake. When she looked overwhelmed and Kathi kind of brought me around as well, I told the doctor, that the previous LTAC facility, basically around the corner, had taken several chest x-rays of Kathi's lungs. If you want, I can go pick them up myself, since I have an MPOA. The doctor agreed, she would order them.

January 6, 2015.

Apparently, Kathi does not have pneumonia, as she is scheduled to be discharged on January 8, 2015. I asked the alternate case manager (first time we've seen one at this place; 'Frances' why or how the decision was made to release Kathi on January 8, when they still had release pending on her white board. Her reply began; "Well, the insurance....". I told her after the third word, she had answered my question. She did not get my response and began telling me again, I stopped her and explained to her, "you answered my question when you said insurance". They're releasing her without completing or beginning some of her scheduled/projected PT exercises. Sometimes, the insurance companies seem to drive decisions based on an aggregate assessment; one not based on reality and of course the shareholders, who absolutely have no clue – so much for the Hippocratic Oath. This is also inefficient approach, because it has been my family's experience, that the patient is back in the hospital within a week. Now for me, my concerns have been accelerated:

- Discharge Instructions
  - o Home healthcare – PT/OT How many days per week?
  - o Special Equipment
    - Oxygen!!! How/where to get the equipment/ replacement tanks
    - Walker
    - More powerful nebulizer for her breathing treatments
- Doctor follow-ups
  - o Cardio
  - o Pulmonary
  - o Infectious Disease
  - o New PCP
  - o Prescription/Meds

January 7, 2015.

I suppose this particular chapter is coming to a close. I'm very anxious about Kathi coming home at this time. Afraid is probably a better word. When the home healthcare is not here and something happens, what then? I'm not prepared. I have not had anyone to talk to through this. I realized this morning, that like Mary; "I have kept these things in my heart"[22]. I need to go to Home Depot and get a hand held shower wand/head for Kathi.

One thing this has taught me, "tried my patience", is to be explicit and concise in my communications. Most do not seem to get or care about my innuendoes, sarcasm or sidehanded comments. It only generates more misunderstanding, and questions which only infuriates me more, when I have to explain what I meant. Hearkens back to that old adage; "KISS". What's an adage? Catch my drift? I did not think so.

And to add flavor to my frustration, I went looking for the case manager, at 4:20PM in an attempt to catch them before closing time and to get some semblance of instructions for tomorrow's discharge. She was on phone call, so was asked by another case manager to wait in their waiting/reception area. About 10 minutes later, I was asked to come assist the case manager.

She happened to be on the phone with insurance company, and was being helped by 'Amor'. Amor had just come online, while Susan waited for about 50 minutes in the cue. So, Amor, apparently an orientee herself began leading us down her process sheet. We made it to the third question (each answer required Amor to put us on hold), which was not relevant to obtaining/assigning a new PCP. The question had to do with, why is the patient having surgery? So, it was a good thing I arrived when I did, hindsight, I should've gone much earlier and to be part of the conversation at the end of the day; the day before being discharged. It was a good thing too, since the case manager was attempting to obtain a new PCP for Kathi.

I immediately asked Amor what does that have to do with getting a new PCP? We were promptly put on hold and she came back apologizing that she was just following her process sheet, which had a series of questions. I told Amor I was a retired Federal Employee. Once again, put on hold, when Amor came back, she told us, she was the wrong department and would give us the 'right' number. The case manager then did a smart thing and asked Amor if she could transfer us to the right department, making introduction for us. Amor agreed. After several attempts, we wound up with Michael, who told us on picking up the phone, he was the wrong department, but would get us to the right department. His attempts got us to a department which went by the acronym COB, which was answered by Khalisa and she informed us, she was also wrong department. I stepped in again and explained to Khalisa that I was a retired federal employee and was attempting to obtain a specific new PCP, who replaced her old PCP, for my wife who was being discharged tomorrow with follow-up instructions to see her PCP. Khalisa said, "Oh, I can help you with that!" Took five minutes, after the case manager had been on phone for 65 minutes, mostly on hold and seems the case manager probably dialed wrong 800# to begin with. As it was, I got back to Kathi's room at 5:45PM.

10. Home

January 8, 2015. Independence Day!

Home Health Care Day One?

W e had scheduled discharge for 1:00 PM, so as to avoid rush hour traffic. Turns out, process included certain equipment to be delivered to the rehab facility before discharge, such as a portable oxygen tank and a walker. Equipment company said they would deliver between 1 and 5 pm, sounds like the cable company. Some more concerns for me included:

- Nurse setting up home visit appointment(s)
- Equipment company setting up deliveries
  - o Shower Seat
  - o Raised Toilet seat
- Pharmacist setting up prescriptions
- Plan for medical equipment area at the house–me
- New shower head – me
- A/C Filters–me

Oxygen tank and walker were delivered at 5:15PM. I'm going to guess, this has to do with communication or lack of it. The equipment rep said the oxygen tank was good for 2 hours and he told us to call them when we were leaving the rehab facility, so we could arrive at approximately the same time. So much for our planned discharge of 1:00 PM for the purpose of missing rush hour traffic. Kathi was discharged at 5:35 PM, so the tank clock began ticking in our minds and we were right in the middle of rush hour. Not so much as a good bye from the case manager. At least the nurse faxed the prescriptions to our pharmacy, as they (rehab facility) could not call them in, this was accomplished because I asked the question. I decided just to drive the streets instead of the freeway, at least the streets constantly moved, except when there was a stop light and they were less congested. Along the way, I knew my Kathi was coming back, as she asked why I was taking a certain street instead of staying on the street I was on.

The equipment was to be delivered in two lots. First lot was delivered to the rehab facility with the second lot to be delivered to the house, when we got home. Along the way, I attempted to call the equipment company, staying within the newly passed city ordinance of hands free and I was good until my phone call got to the options menu; I could not select '2' by voice, so I hung up. Wheels turning.....Kathi has her cell phone! I asked Kathi to call the number, which I gave her, she talked to live person, but Kathi became concerned because even though she had dialed a local number; the live person was in Tucson, AZ. It got straightened out and we arrived home at 6:55PM. Got Kathi inside and comfortable.

After getting home, unpacking the truck, reheating spaghetti that her BFF had made and we were finishing up eating when I received call from equipment company at 7:25PM saying they would be at the house in about 30 minutes. I began getting anxious explaining to him that I don't think we can wait that long as we had a two-hour tank, which would probably be expiring in 10 minutes or so. The gentleman verified that Kathi was set at 2 liters and I said yes and he said that tank is good for 4.5 hours. I relaxed. Ok.

The second lot consisted of an oxygen generator, which separates the oxygen from the ambient air, 6 more portable tanks and a nebulizer. That took until about 8:45PM, which included our crash course. Thank goodness, the pharmacy stays open until 10:00 PM. I went and picked up fourteen prescriptions, did a little grocery shopping. Got home at 10:00 PM, Kathi was spent and I got her into bed, but my lower back was killing me. Thank you BFF for the spaghetti!

January 9, 2015.

Turns out the Xopenex was not part of the 14 items I picked up last night. So I called the pharmacy, turns out they 'missed' it and 'Larry' said they would get right on it and deliver it to the house! I told him thank you!

One of the other items lidocaine patch was not approved by insurance, because it required a pre-authorization from Kathi's PCP. (The hospital doctor is not good enough?). Course, I was told this at 9:15 PM and the insurance company's 'customer service' is unavailable to discuss at that time of day. Fortunately another pain medicine was issued, hopefully that will suffice for Kathi. Apparently, they are not aware or care that Kathi had to have another PCP assigned less than 24 hours earlier. We have a process to follow. Sometimes the process is inefficient, because of the inherent delays and do-overs the process may cause, actually increases overhead costs because you have to hire additional people/resources to implement, monitor and track all the redundant, no-value added processes and the forgotten part by the shareholders is the patient, whether he/she lives/dies is of no import to the bottom line. No wonder many physicians are not accepting or participating in insurance plans. Once again, who is it that actually suffers? You are forsaking the patient for the sake of the process. Perhaps there is a method to this madness – creates additional stress on the caregiver, generating additional revenues through created/new medical conditions, medical requirements.

Besides the weather keeping us hunkered down all day; I'm pretty much the nurse 24/7 until the home health care starts showing up on Monday.

The home healthcare (HHC) admit nurse did visit us today for 2.5 hours, I think she was a little overwhelmed by Kathi's conditions. A couple of things that concerned the HHC nurse was Kathi's low BP and pulse ox. She mentioned life alert so that Kathi would have a button to push for 911.

HEB delivered the Xopenex to the door!

I also spent an hour and a half on the phone with an 'objective' insurance case manager. I told her I was not happy with the service I was receiving and the lack of information relative to Kathi's care on 'my portal'.

January 10, 2015.

Sleeping next to Kathi last night listening to her (shallow) breathing. When she was snoring, it was good, I knew at least she was breathing. And go figure, she wakes me up (I already am), when 'my' snoring wakes her up. Plus, when she got up to use the restroom, which was often, this also disturbed me as I was waiting for her to fall.

I chose not to serve at Mass this week-end, because I did not feel I could leave Kathi. I hope I do not go to hell for that. Monica, our next door neighbor will be bringing us communion tomorrow. I am tired, hope I sleep tonight.

Heavenly Father, watch over, protect us and keep us safe! I did fix the dishwasher and install Kathi's shower wand today.

January 11, 2015.

The Baptism of the Lord! I would've had a fair homily, based on personal witness, not of the Lord's Baptism, but personal experiences; however it is not about me. Kathi got up earlier (8:30 A.M.) to do her breathing treatment, take her morning meds including the iron, which can only be taken after eating. She is staying awake until Monica brings us communion at 10:30. By the way, Kathi took her first shower at home in over 3 months; last night.

January 12, 2015.

Kathi is still home. HHC nurse has checked her vitals and drew blood for her International Normalized Ratio (INR) check. This is a blood test to determine the blood's clotting ability. Her INR is 1.4, so she has called the cardiologist to receive Coumadin dose for Kathi. We reminded the nurse that she must talk to the doctor and not receive orders from his nurse. Instructions from the cardiologist's nurse was for 3 mg today through Wednesday, then 2 mg Thursday through Sunday and "we'll" check INR again on Monday. Being that Kathi is in Afib, she runs the risk of blood clots, which can cause a stroke; so the desire is to keep her blood 'thin' and reduce that risk through the adminis-tration of Coumadin, Warfarin or Jantoven to name a few of the blood thinner (anticoagulant) medicines on the market. The ideal for Kathi is to be between 2 to 3.

Kathi began her PT and OT in earnest today as 'Ryan' evaluated her for PT and gave her a few exercises, keeping in mind her recent heart surgery and her limitations due to that. Her OT nurse (evaluator), was from our Sunday night Knights of Columbus bowling league! What a pleasant surprise. She provided some tips regarding household safety and precautions. Since Kathi currently has difficulty rising from a sitting position, Cathy recommended adding four inches to her recliner. After looking at it, I thought perhaps cutting up a 4"X4" and placing a piece of plywood on top of it to serve as a more stable platform to screw to the chair's runners. However, upon further consideration I thought the increase in height might change the center of gravity for the chair making it top heavy, because it was not designed to be raised four inches. That would just add a safety risk. I will review other options. Additionally, Cathy talked about adding grab bars at various places in the house, such as for getting out of the sunken living room/den and especially the bathroom /shower stall and floor mats designed for non-slip. I went out and purchased those, we'll see how they work.

January 13, 2015.

Today is an observation of how far Kathi has come just in the short five days she has been home.

- She dressed herself for PT
- She carried her dish to the kitchen sink by herself
- I had left a bread board in the kitchen sink and she washed it

- She is walking unassisted (or furniture surfing as her PT evaluator called it) to the restroom and to get her meds; pushing me out of the way, she wants to do it!

- Today her BP has remained good and high (for her) enabling her to continue her anti-arrhythmia medicine for two days in a row!

- She had long conversations with her girlfriends on the phone today

- She reminded me about needing referrals for her doctors. I'm glad she did and cannot believe I thought it was automatic just because it was on the hospital discharge instructions. We went through this in August for crying out loud, even though we were tracking it and staying on top of the referrals. We were in 6 week insurance and PCP staff inefficiency imposed hiatus.

- We have watched 3 Spurs games since she has come home, including tonight. I told Kathi these were the first games I've watched this season. I'm surprised too since the first one we watched was real nail-biter; I was worried about Kathi's heart.

January 14, 2015.

The nurse visited again today, they are scheduled three times a week and took Kathi's vitals. There was no requirement for INR check. I called the PCP office to obtain referrals for the specialist's visits, her pulmonologist is tomorrow, so this is exciting ensuring the referral occurs in a timely manner, does not matter that I have been sitting on the request. We also have to fill out the pulmonologist's new patient forms, it's a 9 page document and yes they were faxed to the house last week.

January 15, 2015.

We arrived at the pulmonologist's office early, a little confusing at first, since it was in a tower and the dispatch service did not know anything about the parking arrangements. The only entrance I could see without going into the parking lot (pay) had a slight incline about 50 feet into the front entrance. So I parked the truck at the entrance, turned it off and took the keys (Kathi has a habit of leaning on the door locks when she gets in/out of the truck) got the walker from behind my seat, then walked around and took out the oxygen bottle from behind her seat, which I had secured the holder to her headrest with a short bungee cord. Then I helped her out of the truck, handing her cannula to her, helped up the ramp through the entry door and to a sitting place in front of the elevators; the doctor's office was on the 6ᵗʰ floor. I went back to the truck, circled back around the entry and through the parking lot entry and turns out there was a parking lot at the back of the tower and the elevators were equidistant from either doorway.

The referral had not quite gotten there when we checked in, but the staff was patient and very helpful in working with the PCP's office and insurance company making sure it got done before we left. The doctor was happy to see her, telling her she was amazing and had come a long way. He asked about the oxygen saying he did not think she needed it when she was just sitting down watching television and the like. He had his nurse give her a 6 minute walk test, checking her pulse/ox every minute along the way and Kathi did this test without the walker for 277M in the hallway. After reviewing the test, he verified that she did not need the oxygen when she was in resting mode. He also took some x-rays, which he reviewed with us and her lungs looked a lot cleaner, not so cluttered with opaqueness, than they have in a long, long time. He also talked about her Coumadin, said it did not make much sense to maintain the same dosage, when the INR was low, so he raised to 5 mg until Monday when her INR would be taken again. He wanted a follow-up within 4-6 weeks, I told him we originally had one scheduled for Feb 23 from the hospital, so he said if that is still on his calendar, let's go with that. He also gave Kathi a prescription for the smaller/ lighter oxygen bottles.

We got home about 11:00 A.M., on the way I stopped at a drive-through, Kathi wanted some crispy tacos, and I got breakfast tacos. Kathi passed her swallow test and took a long nap.

January 16, 2015. (Happy Birthday to me!)

Today, we were visited by the social worker, not sure why, but when I asked the question, it is a formality process with all new patients incurring home health care. 'Beatriz' told us about various agencies who can help us if we need assistance with normal household duties, such as washing dishes, cooking, just being present, which can be short-term or long-term. She asked if we were veterans, I told her I was and she said the VA offers attendant benefits, which I did not know about. The one question I had was about obtaining a disabled parking permit, she gave an overview of the process including costs. She emailed some informational brochures later in the day. Of course, we do not qualify for most of the services because of my income and/or we own property.

January 17, 2015.

I was in class most of the day for my Level II Catechist certification. Kathi had visitors then rested most of the day. Her visitors saw to Kathi's care and meals while I was in class.

January 18, 2015.

I was on schedule for the 9:00, 11:00 A.M. and 5:30 P.M. Masses. I served at the 9:00 and 11:00 A.M. providing a homily on being called for the 2nd Sunday of Ordinary Time readings in Cycle B.

Readings:

1 Samuel 3:3B-10, 19

1 Cor 6:13C-15A, 17-20

Psalms: 40

John 1:35-42

Introduction

Today is a Sunday of calling. We hear of Samuel's calling. St. Paul in his letter to the Corinthians of their calling and in the Gospel several of John the Baptist's disciples hear the calling of Jesus and act on it by following Him; including Andrew and his brother Simon Peter. The Word is also calling you and me.

Move 1

How quickly do we respond, when we are called? There were a few throughout Scripture who were not quite as responsive as Samuel or Andrew and Simon.

Jacob wrestled all night with God and was named Israel. Jonah was terrified to proclaim to the people of Nineveh, eventually God wore him down, he relented and God spoke through him and the people of Nineveh, listened to him, repented of their sins and wicked ways, turning back to God. Even Moses, a fine field general for Pharoah's army, was humbled before the Lord and did not think himself worthy.

St. Paul also had his hands full with the Corinthians. They were living in a bustling and diverse seaport city which enjoyed a thriving trade commerce. The city of Corinth was filled with idol worship, materialism and secularism and all sorts of distractions to the keep the Church of Corinth sidetracked.

What is our usual response when we hear that call? "I do not have the talent or gift required for that mission". Or "I am not worthy to do the Lord's work". God provides us with gifts and talents to do His will. Some are hidden until it is time that He wishes to reveal them.

Move 2

I have to share with you my own call, which I first heard as a young child hearing the Gospel of Matthew chapter 4, verse 19; He said to them, "Come after me and I will make you fishers of men". It took nearly 35 years to say yes after sitting in the pews of this Church for 10 years watching my own family receive the Sacraments. Every Sunday, Father Pat's homilies were talking directly to me, in my heart, a heart that I did not think I had. I accepted the faith and came home as a convert. And when I came up to the Altar that Easter vigil in 1992, I believe that God was using Fr. Pat as His voice again, when he asked me; "What took you so long?".

From that point, it has been another 23 years to be standing here as God's servant for you.

St. Paul tells us that our body is not our own and is meant for the Lord and the Lord for our body. We are temples of the Holy Spirit and we are responsible for keeping this temple clean and healthy. We have been set free by sharing in His Baptism, which we heard about last Sunday and by accepting the Cross. We are no longer slaves to the devil and his sin. Yet God does call us to evangelize to the ends of the earth, baptizing in the name of the Father, Son and Holy Spirit, teaching all nations what He has commanded us, working for the salvation of souls.

Move 3

Jesus tells us not to be afraid when we pick up our crosses and follow Him. His yoke is easy and burden light when we let go of our burdens at the foot of the Cross.

We are not to be afraid, like Mary when she said yes in obedience to her call. Each of us have a place in God's plan. When we say yes, listening to that 'little voice' like Elijah. What that yes means will be revealed to you and I as God wills.

We have become a member of Christ's body through our Baptism. We are to glorify God in our bodies and actions. As the Lord reminds us in Matthew 5:16; "…that they may see your good works and give glory to your Father who is in Heaven".

Conclusion

John the Baptist has pointed Jesus out to us in the 2nd Verse of today's Gospel; "Behold the Lamb of God!". When Jesus turns to you and I and asks, "What do you seek?". As we approach the table of the Eucharist, let our hearts be open and echo the Psalmist's response: "Here am I, Lord, I come to do your will.

Kathi was not feeling that well when I arrived home after the 11:00 A.M. Mass and I called in, letting the priest know I would not be there for the 5:30 P.M. Mass.

January 20, 2015.

Today is first follow-up with Kathi's new PCP. It was more of a getting to know you visit, plus a new round of lab work. While we were in the lab waiting area, Kathi had just went into the lab, when her old PCP walks in (he quit and sold his practice/patients to Kathi's new PCP and became a hospitalist), specifically to see Kathi. Many emotions came rushing back upon me when I saw him, as they are while I'm writing this. Once again, I told him thank you and in his humility, he said it had nothing to do with him. But, he did begin the recovery process with Kathi. He went into the lab and visited with Kathi, then came back out to the waiting area and sat with me, telling me she's amazing and miraculous! I told him that is the word.

January 21, 2015. Trinity's Birthday!

What I'm noticing is that Kathi's modus operandi (mo) is the same, but not quite as pronounced as it was before her long hospitalization, she'll have one good day, then have to rest for a couple of days. She is still having difficulty breathing and her pulse/ox is in the 70s when Kathi is not using the oxygen.

Now that Kathi is home and I repeat; Home Health Care is not here 24/7, I believe I'm losing more sleep than when she was in the hospital. I'm sleeping with one eye/ear open, listening to her every noise or lack of any.

You may have noticed within this chapter and book, the gamut of emotions, which might occur within any given day and during this entire period.

11. The Drain

Your physiological state takes a beating as the days, weeks and months go by with nary a relief or respite in site, as doctor upon doctor is 'puzzled' and your loved one presents them an 'interesting' case, while they appear ill prepared to solve. Each caregiver, of course will experience different effects on their physique and psyche. There is not a cookie-cutter approach we can take in caring for the caregiver or the patient. We can learn from the professional caregivers, the doctors, the nurses and assisting staff who care for patients day in/day out, 12 hour shifts at a time. How do they cope with the constant barrage for attention, and information dissemination and the ultimate burden, for which they have been trained?

I am attempting to provide this for those of us not trained in care-giving, particularly those of us where the vocation is dropped in our lap and/or we did not heed the warning signs.

Physical

Because you have been selected to be your loved one's caregiver, your physical well-being becomes just as important to maintain. How do you do that? When your entire day or night is spent at your loved one's bedside. You must set aside time for you. Even when you are at the hospital(s), take a break, wear tennis/walking shoes and comfortable clothes; walk around the outside of the hospital, if it's inclement weather, walk the halls of the hospital and/or up and down the stairwells. Your loved one should be resting and recuperating. Do not make excuses, take care of yourself. When you go home in the evening, take a walk around the neighborhood. If the hospital is not in your hometown and you're staying at a hotel/motel, make sure the amenities include a workout facility. Pack your workout clothes, a swimsuit.

Yes, I'm not going to sugarcoat this; being a caregiver is very tiring. When you get home after a full day at the hospital waiting on the doctors charged with the care of your loved one, making their rounds; you are worn out. Every day. Yet, you must make time for yourself, ensuring your physical well-being by exercising and I do not mean 12 ounce curls. Exercising your eyes in front of the TV does not fill the bill either. You can do that later, it's great for putting you to sleep, if you're having trouble doing that.

Some days you are so tired, getting up the next day seems an insurmountable challenge. But, if you do not get up and ensure your loved one is being cared for, who will?

Exercise

This is for the caregiver, more than for anyone else during your time as a caregiver. It does not necessarily require three hours at the gym every day. Something as simple as taking a walk in your neighborhood could be sufficient, the time of day and type of exercise is up to you. What is important is that you take this time for yourself, to ensure you remain healthy enough to fulfill your role as the caregiver. Taking the time 'away' from being a caregiver is important for you as the caregiver to facilitate physical, mental, physiologic and emotional health and stability. Try to physically and mentally remove yourself during this time from caregiving thoughts and emotions, attempt to clear the slate and THINK about nothing except recharging your own batteries. Do not take the time away by sitting in front of the television or computer; there is/will be plenty of time for that as it is while you are 'sitting' with your loved one. They will be sleeping a lot on their own as their body recovers and recuperates and is aided by chemicals prescribed by the experts.

Mental

I am fortunate that I am a consultant and my 'job' is reading and writing for my clients, which I can do from most anywhere, as long as I have my laptop and my clients allow it. Or perhaps your employer will allow telecommuting for a time. This is how I mentally took a break, even while I was in Kathi's various hospital rooms. She knew

I was there and if a doctor making rounds showed up; I was there to hear the latest plan. When she was not eating, I used that tray on wheels; sometimes the staff would bring an extra one into the room for my laptop. Otherwise, it was on my lap. Those visitor chairs in the patient's room are not the most comfortable, so please refer to physical well-being above.

If your job does not allow that, bring a book to read, a (quiet) game to play, crossword puzzle, Sudoku, or watch a movie on your tablet/laptop. Whatever you do to take your mind off things, bring that medium with you to the hospital, which does not include an ice chest, you need to be as sharp as possible. Bring water and change. There were vending machines in all the hospitals.

There will be plenty of time for you to take that mental break. This time around, Kathi was basically out for the first nine days and the only way for her to gain strength was to rest and her body did this automatically. So while she was resting, I was working, reading or transcribing my notes and taking occasional walks around the facilities.

Emotional

This is probably the most daunting challenge, having a place to release the emotions. You can sometimes release the emotions by physically working out. I used to have a speed bag (the little punching bag that boxers use for practice) in my garage; I also had a bicycle on a training stand, so I could peddle in place, while listening to my iPod.

Walking, jogging, playing racquetball, riding your bicycle or a pickup game of basketball will definitely provide that physical work-out and relieve some of the emotional stress you are experiencing at this time of your life. Some of these activities at my age are prohibitive, particularly since I tore my meniscus (subsequently removed) in my left knee three years ago playing third base. Granted, this type of release is not for everyone, the important thing to focus on is what form of relief works for you. Again, the bottle or mind-numbing drugs (legal or otherwise) are not beneficial and lead to other problems. You, as caregiver, have to be present for your loved one. A physical exertion will provide emotional relief.

You can also relieve some of the emotions by reading a good book; whatever genre you prefer. My personal favorites are Church history and books on theology. I've also read what I call entertainment novels, such as current spy books.

Emotions

However, there will still remain emotions, for that you need someone to talk to, who is detached from your tragedy, someone who can provide an objective response to your situation. A place to start might be the hospital chaplain, if you feel the need to 'vent'. The hospital chaplain would have access to or information relating to additional resources you might require, depending upon your circumstances. They have been trained to provide a resource for the patient and caregiver. Another might be your Church priest, deacon or pastor; who could be available for you, as well as provide additional counseling resource services.

As much as you have to be the rock and maintain your composure, there are times when the overwhelming feeling washes over you. Your eyes well up, you catch your breath, because for a picosecond, that thought of you alone without her encompasses your entire being and almost brings you to your knees. This will happen at any time day or night or in any place, whether you are shopping in the grocery store, driving your truck, sitting in Church or waking up in the middle of the night. I cannot tell you what brings it on. All I can tell you is that it happens and it contains that same feeling of helplessness sitting in the ICU room when she mouths the words "Help Me!". Perhaps because of your connectedness to her, you are receiving across the neuro-synapses, a small smidgeon of what she is feeling as she is dying.

Frustration

This is as much frustration with the healthcare industry as it is with family and friends. With all the circumstances surrounding your loved one, your loved ones wear you out! Sometimes I don't like half the folks I love.[23] An overview of what transpired in the first few days and how I felt follows and are copies of emails, which I sent out to the prayer warriors, family and friends distribution list:

October 3, 2014.

Can you pass to Delia that her Rosary was blessed and that Kathi has clutched it in her right hand since 2:00 pm today, when I presented it to her. Today, April, one of our nieces in NYC called and told Kathi she loved her, that she and a group of friends prayed a Rosary for Kathi today at St. Patrick's Cathedral. This reminded me that I had a Rosary for Kathi.

Praise God! She came out of the anesthesia with a big smile; just like Msgr. Pat said she would. She's squeezing hands hard, not talking (yet), but definitely communicating and did I say she was smiling, with those bright, sparkly eyes.

I just spoke with Dr. S (acute care doctor for the hospital ICU), Kathi is making positive improvement, it will probably be Monday before she is off the ventilator. What Dr. S is doing when he comes to check on Kathi is turning down the percentage that the machine works (and it is always a backup), Kathi is at about 35 %. He also said it may be rough when they do take her off the machine. But right now, they are focusing on the endocarditis (infection in her heart), and they are waiting on the culture to come back that will tell them which bug it is. He mentioned 3, the only one I remember is sepsis, that way they will know which antibiotic regimen to implement, but any of the protocol will be a 6 week effort. It's positive; however, she will not be leaving the hospital soon. Good news, not staph! But they have to re-culture to determine what specific bug to counter with what antibiotic.

October 4, 2014.

Thanks, brother. Something got her spooled up, anxious, higher HR, BP and rapid shallow breathing and she was getting frightened and couldn't control it. The docs came in and a few things were tweaked and she's resting now. Tell Richard the staff thank him for his hospitality; you know the same kind he provided us in class sometimes. I probably need to curtail visitors for a few days and let Kathi rest/recover, doctors say she's getting too much stimulus.

October 11, 2014.

Today, there is no change in Kathi's status. The setback 2 days ago was that she got agitated and her circulatory and respiratory systems accelerated and she couldn't control it. The doctor reset the ventilator to 14 from 6. They were slowly weaning her. Her lungs and muscles got tired of working so hard, subsequently she couldn't catch her breath and she spooled up. (That's my term, not a medical term).

No change in status means no change in status. If you do not hear from me, it's because there is nothing to report. No news is no news. I know everyone loves her and is concerned about Kathi's well-being; no less than me and there is a certain feeling of helplessness in not knowing. Also know that what happened to Kathi did not happen in 30 minutes nor is it going to take 30 minutes to fix–life does not follow the structure or resolution of a TV show. Kathi has an awesome staff of doctors and nurses who are devoted to her care with all the modern tools at their disposal. I am not a 24/7 News service, I will not be providing endless rambling commentary, based on conjecture, speculation, hyperbole or guessing. If you are expecting that or seeking details; wait for the book. Which I am writing and Kathi has asked me to, but I am not going to provide my daily log about Kathi's health, which goes back several years, in this medium, in an email or blog site. Yes, there is a bit of emotion here. I love you for loving Kathi; that has always been easy. Know that she is still fighting and what she is fighting is comprehensive, not one isolated issue. In the meantime–no news is no news.

Loved Ones

They mean well wanting to know all the details and that is who we are as a species, having that ineluctable desire to know. Today, it is even more so, as we have to know everything that is going on every second, every minute, every day. And because of that we experience the phenomenon of information overload, which leads to road rage and jumping off buildings. I know, a little melodramatic. However, as the caregiver, you also become the keeper and distributer of information relative to the patient. This occurs by design and default. And it may become a maddening circumstance which feeds the drain in a circular flow. You distribute and offer the information as information, not as a debate invitation. You immediately receive questions from all angles wanting more information and details. As an example, in your 'report', you might add a statement about the doctor made a decision for her care based on her existing conditions. You may get an immediate response wanting you to speculate on why the doctor made that decision. This makes it particularly frustrating for you, when: (1) you gave them the information they needed (2) you are not a 24 hour news service (3) you are not trained in the medical profession to provide that speculation. You are attempting to be a caregiver and you are trying to be nice by providing all the loved and not so loved ones periodic updates on the patient. What is infuriating is that sometimes there is no news to report. And that is what you have to impart to them; no news is no news. Sometimes the news is nunya (none of your business) outside the 'inner circle', if there is one, or on a need to know basis. And Lord knows you have to be considerate of everyone's feelings, while you are keeping yours in check – this is what helps fuel the stress and helps the drain in all three elements; physical, mental and emotional or the total package: physiologically. And believe me, it wears on you almost as much as watching your loved one waste away daily.

12. Employment

For sanity's sake, it is important you maintain activity which helps you focus on something besides the hospital. My distraction is my work, which for all intents and purposes appears to be my hobby. I have been fortunate to be able to work from my wife's hospital room while she is resting and recuperating and at the same time, be there if she needs something. I'm also there when most of the doctors make their rounds, which enables me to 'be up to speed' on the latest plan for or menace to Kathi's recovery.

From an economic perspective, it is also important, since in my case, my healthcare premiums account for 75% of my 'retirement'. That is why my hobby is to be gainfully employed, but then I like to work and we enjoy some of the extra benefits.

It is imperative you are able to maintain a balance between caring for your loved one, in addition to periodic detachments, which allow for renewal and recharging of your psyche. Again, this particular focus worked for me, as I was able to work from my wife's hospital room.

And, more importantly while being present for my wife, I wanted to be there when the doctors made their rounds. For others, it may be required to have a full, literal detachment by going into the office and attempting to work from there. But, will you really be there? Will every phone call to your desk phone or cell phone make you steadily apprehensive and on edge; anticipating 'that call'? Will your mind wander in meetings to what is happening at the hospital? Will you be effective in the performance of your job? Then, there will be the constant questions from your coworkers relative to your spouse's well-being. You will be the focus of the office that will take you mentally back to the hospital, so the physical detachment may not provide the relief required.

13. Transition

On leaving the synagogue

Jesus entered the house of Simon and Andrew with James and John.

Simon's mother-in-law lay sick with a fever.

They immediately told him about her.

He approached, grasped her hand, and helped her up.

Then the fever left her and she waited on them.

When it was evening, after sunset,

they brought to him all who were ill or possessed by demons.

The whole town was gathered at the door.

He cured many who were sick with various diseases,

and he drove out many demons,

not permitting them to speak because they knew him.

Rising very early before dawn, he left

and went off to a deserted place, where he prayed.

Simon and those who were with him pursued him

and on finding him said, "Everyone is looking for you."

He told them, "Let us go on to the nearby villages

that I may preach there also.

For this purpose have I come."

So he went into their synagogues,

preaching and driving out demons throughout the whole of Galilee.[24]

February 10, 2015

T here is not a conclusion to this story, nor is this a summary. This is more about transition from one stage of life to the next; a dying to oneself and rebirth to a new self, a new life. This transition effects and affects all concerned, most assuredly, the patient and by extension, her loved ones.

When the doctor in Tyler told us in July, that Kathi's life would not necessarily be shortened by the bronchiectasis, but that her quality of life would definitely be impacted by the disease; at the time sounded like so many words from a catchphrase. Echoing across these last 8 months; the words have come home to roost in a challenging dose of reality. The planning of any activity or family event revolves around the physical limitations imposed on the patient.

As an example, Kathi had planned to join her six aunts for their monthly sister's breakfast yesterday. One routine has remained since before this most recent hospitalization. She will participate in one activity, but then will need to spend the next couple of days recovering from that exertion. That being said, Kathi had agreed to celebrate Christmas 2014 this past Sunday afternoon. At the time, and not knowing when she would be actually released from hospital care, Kathi had asked the family to postpone Christmas until she got home; all agreed.

A small silver tree with blue ornaments was still up, along with the five grandchildren's filled stockings on the mantle and a pile of presents in the middle of the living room waiting to be opened greeted our children and their families when they came over about 2:00 P.M. As much as Kathi wanted to, she was unable to pick up or tussle with her grandchildren on her lap; but there was definitely a light in her eyes as her 3 year old grandson came running in to greet her, simultaneously throwing his present for her to her that she caught! One of our granddaughters asked Kathi if she would be going swimming with them in our pool this summer. Kathi responded with a hopeful "maybe?".

Our family was together for about four hours, and I told them I did not have any meal planned for this event; that was probably selfish on my part, as I was tired with a sore shoulder blade. When they arrived, I was sitting with a heating pad; actually I was sleeping in a sitting position on the couch, when my grandson rang the doorbell. The four hours took its loving toll on Kathi; she awoke on Monday to get ready for sister's breakfast, but she did not feel well at all and told me to call her aunt who was coming to pick her up. Kathi slept all day until the 5:00 PM news. I was apprehensive about this outing anyway. Am I being too protective? Am I holding her back?

Kathi is bound and determined; she is becoming more independent, but she is definitely getting 'cabin' fever. Her only outings have been to doctors' appointments. On Sunday, she actually mentioned, "maybe we can go to the coast next weekend". She recognizes she would not be able to go to the beach, but she would be very happy to sit on our 'other' back porch. And since my truck has an AC outlet, we could carry the oxygen generator with us in the truck and hook it up in the condo with her 50 foot tether.

This transition represents a change in our lifestyle. The rodeo is in town in two days and my brother-in-law asked if I wanted to attend one of the events with him, but I am unable to justify leaving Kathi alone while I go have fun. I am not trying to come across as a martyr; only trying to emphasize how your routines as you knew them are going to experience some revision. We are certainly catching up on watching our Spurs, especially now they are on the rodeo roadtrip and the first few games are going through the East, so the games are coming on earlier! You begin to appreciate the simpler things in this life, you take the time to "smell the roses and blow out the candles". Kathi has been very excited to sit on our back porch and I have to clean the debris off the glider, so she can sit on it.

Your event planning is going to be more 'spontaneous' and will be predicated on how the patient feels. Your social calendar will revolve around her limitations. Which, in and of itself is not a bad thing. We have been given an opportunity to renew our relationship in a much closer bond. We have drawn closer together in centering our lives in God. Right now, I am her eyes and ears to the outside world, but at the same time, I'm only as far away as the next room.

This transition represents a brave new world as you are happy beyond words that your soul mate, best friend and confidant is still sharing this side of heaven with you. Any activity, no matter how seemingly inane or trivial it may appear to 'outsiders'; is an indescribable blessing. The question does remain as a prayer for wisdom and understanding of God's plan. Now, that my love and I are beginning to return to a semblance of our former lifestyle and what each day brings; "what is our mission?". We pray and Kathi prays for healing of her bronchiectasis. What we do in the meantime is geared towards Kathi's recovery and healing. We manage 'baby' steps and revel in the small successes occurring every day, praising God's goodness with every step. Where will our renewed ministry take us? Into hospitals, LTACs, nursing homes, rehabilitation facilities, hospices, homebound?

The purpose of this entry, which must have something to do with the Season of Lent and the leanings toward reflection and meditation, has more to do with my faith and why I have chosen the Catholic faith. I will attempt to do this in a few short sentences.

Over the last nearly six decades, I have done a lot of soul searching. In my early and adolescent years, I truly believed in the God and Jesus of the Bible. I wanted to be a "fisher of men", as I had heard so often in Church as a child. I also believed you could live the Beatitudes and would be disappointed more often than not, when that was not an everyday reality for most.

Then, one of those 'life events' (sorry for the vernacular, because it makes light of a tragedy in the family and I'm not alone in having experienced this) occur which make you stop in your tracks and re-evaluate your belief system. I blamed God for taking my mother away to heaven and I knew that is where she went.

Once that grief subsided somewhat or I pushed it down into the depths of my heart, which amazingly, I still do not seem to have access to; I began going to Church with my new stepmom, joined the youth group (to meet girls) and ventured out with school friends to their places of worship and their youth groups. I guess they must have seen something in me which I still do not recognize. Servant leader? More than that, is I learned about the faith(s) and denomination(s) beliefs and traditions. And that is why I continued my search:

- The faith did not feel right to me
- I was still harboring anger against God.

In my teen and early adult years, I really searched the cosmic unknown for that Supreme Being. And towards the end of that period, I met Kathi, who told me you do not need any of that! All you need is Love!

Once I embraced the Catholic faith in my fortieth year (I knew before then), I began to experience and witness personal blessings, graces and miracles, in addition to those of others. And in hindsight, I recognized those same miracles and blessings in events which occurred in my family prior to my conversion as God's hand steering me to Him.

Ultimately, the transition becomes or has become a matter of personal transformation, a continuing metanoia or conversion of my heart and faith. A continued 'dying' to my old self. During this entire journey, my faith has been sustained and maintained through my belief in the Father, Son and Holy Spirit. I recognize the Catholic Church has experienced its own scandals and foibles throughout its history up through today. However, I also recognize the Church of Christ established on the Apostle St. Peter resides within the Catholic Church and the Holy Spirit which gave birth to the Church at Pentecost is the glue which holds the Catholic Church together, through its trials and tribulations caused by man. The Church stands as the visible testament to God in our history.

Kathi and I look to the Love of Jesus to guide us, the Holy Spirit to strengthen our hearts and the Will of God to embrace us with perseverance and witness.

14. Epilogue

December 23, 2014.

My son's 35th birthday is today. Wish him a happy birthday. Today marks 90 days (ago) that Kathi entered the hospital.

This past Friday (the day Kathi took her first shower in over 3 months), the evaluator from the rehab facility visited Kathi. She had heard what the current facility was saying relative to how long Kathi would require in this physical rehab facility; a couple of weeks. The evaluator gave us her assessment that it would be longer and did not put a time period on Kathi's intensive PT/OT. Kathi has to relearn everything that we take for granted, such as getting dressed, which she has not done yet or even getting out of bed, going to the bathroom. Being a retired Dental Hygienist, she is brushing her teeth (in bed), so someone else has to get her toothbrush/paste and set it up for her and clean it up when she is finished.

We learned on Sunday, the cardiologist stopped the anti-arrhythmia medicine she was taking. He said it was not doing what it was supposed to do; and her heart will always be out of rhythm. Of course, I did not want to hear this, yes I got angry in my way. Two questions came to me; (1) Are you going to prescribe a replacement anti-arrhythmia? (2) Going in, we knew the first 2 ablations did not work; why did we do it a third time? (This was a repeat of question I asked prior to her heart surgery, when they told me they were going to perform this cryo-maze [internal ablation – Dr. Sean's definition] procedure in addition to her mitral valve replacement). The cardiologist on Sunday did say Kathi was amazing.

Yesterday, Kathi had extensive PT/OT, which wore her out for the afternoon sessions. She also had the foley removed yesterday Hurray! – a little more 'independence', as long as the nurses answer the call button in time. The only tube remaining is the oxygen cannula; which will probably remain. All the pulmonologists who have seen Kathi in these past 90 days seemed surprised that she did not already have an oxygen tank at home, considering the condition of her lungs.

As of late yesterday afternoon/evening, the insurance company had not yet 'approved' Kathi's transfer to the rehab facility. They've had this request since Thursday. Many times, it is the language and use or omission of key terms and definitions (that's for the Case Manager to resolve). Kathi and I are also citing the holiday season for the delay. A good segue into why I'm writing this today.

This came to me yesterday morning and has not released me, so I figured I'd better put it out there. This is the part where I ramble as the gears in my heart and head develop what it is I'm supposed to say.

I'm not making light of the situation that Kathi and our family find ourselves experiencing. So far, Kathi has 'celebrated' a grandson's birthday, her son and daughter-in-law's fifth wedding anniversary, her own 42nd wedding anniversary, a heart surgery (much needed) for thanksgiving, and all four Sundays of Advent in the hospital. She will also spend Christmas, New Year's and quite possibly my birthday next month in the hospital. And she has missed numerous other family get-togethers and severely misses her five grandchildren whom she has not seen or visited with for these past 90 days. There is the possibility of hope, that in the event Kathi moves to the rehab facility, the grandchildren will be able to surround her on Christmas day.

I also want to make it clear; this is how I perceive things. Of course, my perception is based on my faith, belief and value system developed over the course of my lifetime thus far. I am not a 'victim' of my environment. That development has occurred due in no small part to my upbringing, by the Church, my parents, grandparents, those I have admired near and far and whose paths I have crossed over time. Present company included.

Today, in the middle of Advent and Christmas seasons, we as a species, look to the hope of our coming Savior. Now, this hope affects and effects the human population of the globe; whether they have been introduced to Jesus or not. God entered man's history in the form of man through Mary. As we prepare every year for Christmas, the rest of the world are witnesses to this miracle, as we re-live and re-tell this salvific, historic event.

There are many who experience a sense of loss internally and externally during this season. Internally, we are seeking that hope, sometimes we feel we have not attained it, leading to a sense of less than hope or hopelessness. And that is a very devastating feeling; while the rest of the world appears joyous (as we should!) and caring for each other and yet, some feel as they live outside of this joy in a void, nothingness.

Those of us who feel the joy and hope of Advent and Christmas have the responsibility and need to be more aware of the people around us and pray for recognition of those seeking. Even in our celebrations of joy and hope, you can see the hurt, loneliness and longing in the eyes, even though the mouth has a plastered/plastic smile emitting canned laughter.

One way to focus is to recognize every day is Christmas, every day is Easter and live our lives accordingly. Will it be easy? No, Scripture tells us so in numerous passages, such as in Matthew 7:14 "How narrow the gate and constricted the road that leads to life. And those who find it are few"[25]. As St. Francis tells us; "Preach the Gospel, and when necessary, use words"[26].

It is a difficult challenge and assignment, because it seems to me, once Christmas is over; it's back to work, school and "everyday" life, until the retailers begin reminding us in August that Christmas is just around the corner. We need to get this season's special gift for that special someone now before they run out. What special gift, God's Love or human touches (as God's Love) are the alone receiving? Perhaps part of the issue is experiencing "everyday" life, while we take for granted the Gift, each individual has received. And during this season of joy and hope, we witness many, loved ones, those we peripherally know and those we do not know – who give that Gift back. And many more in moments of despair cry out for help, which fall in silence, unacknowledged. We need to pray for God's help enabling His servants here on earth to be more aware and cognizant of the loneliness, longing and hurt in others all year round and bring Jesus to them.

One of those I admire from afar is a contemporary desert father at the turn of the 19th century, venerable Charles De Foucauld; whose life's mission was simple: "Love them to Jesus"[27]. And he was following Jesus, who told us in the Gospel of Mark 12:30-31;

30 "You shall love the Lord your God with all your heart, with all your soul, with all your mind, and with all your strength.

31The second is this: 'You shall love your neighbor as yourself.' There is no other commandment greater than these."[28].

We are witnessing Pope Francis in his reaching out to other religions; there are those who are misinterpreting this 'ecumenism' and he is being persecuted for following Jesus; Matthew 5:12[29]. Pope Francis is simply responding to the Great Commission as Jesus sent us all in Matthew 28:18-20;

18 Then Jesus approached and said to them, "All power in heaven and on earth has been given to me.

19 Go, therefore, and make disciples of all nations, baptizing them in the name of the Father, and of the Son, and of the Holy Spirit,

20 teaching them to observe all that I have commanded you. And behold, I am with you always, until the end of the age."[30]

These past 90 days have been a personal season of Advent for me; as our family has experienced parallel seasons of sorrow, joy and hope, sometimes in the same day. There were times, I felt Kathi was not coming home ("O, you of little faith!, why did you doubt". Matthew 14:31[31]). She is not home yet, but your prayers and doctors' prognosis have helped me in my "unbelief" (Mark 9:24: Then the boy's father cried out, "I do believe, help my unbelief"[32]).

What I have witnessed in these last 90 days has presented me with an observation first-hand; there are many who are in the hospitals, whose only physical contact with the outside world are their doctors, nurses and staff. The TV does not count. There are two patients who left Kathi's hallway yesterday for their heavenly home, one in the morning and one in the afternoon. Family, friends were not around. The parking lot (free parking) for a 72 bed facility is relatively empty on the weekends. Reminds me of the Elton John song from the album of the same name: Madman Across the Water.

I want to thank everyone for your prayers, I ask that you continue praying for Kathi's continued recovery and healing, developing her strength and motor skills so she may return home in the New Year. I also ask that you pray for those who are not feeling loved or alone.

God Bless You!

But he said to them, "It is I. Do not be afraid."[33]

Merry Christmas!

GLOSSARY

A

Ablation: Removal or excision. Ablation is usually carried out surgically. For example, surgical removal of the thyroid gland (a total thyroidectomy) is ablation of the thyroid.

Arterial Blood Gases: An arterial blood gas (ABG) test measures the acidity (pH) and the levels of oxygen and carbon dioxide in the blood from an artery.

Acute Respiratory Distress Syndrome (ARDS): Acute respiratory distress syndrome (ARDS) is a lung problem. It happens when fluid builds up in the lungs, causing breathing failure and low oxygen levels in the blood.

Amyloidosis: Amyloidosis is a systemic disorder that is classified into several types. The different types of systemic amyloidosis are sometimes classified as primary, secondary or familial (hereditary). Primary amyloidosis (also called AL) is the most common type of systemic amyloidosis. AL results from an abnormality (dyscrasia) of plasma cells in the bone marrow and is closely related to multiple myeloma.

Antiarrhythmic Medicines for Atrial Fibrillation: Antiarrhythmic medicines help return the heart to its normal sinus rhythm, maintain the rhythm after it has been achieved, and/or reduce the heart rate while you are in atrial fibrillation.

Generic Name	Brand Name
amiodarone	Cordarone, Pacerone
disopyramide	Norpace
dofetilide	Tikosyn
dronedarone	Multaq
flecainide	Tambocor
procainamide	
propafenone	Rythmol
quinidine	
sotalol	Betapace AF

Antithyroid Medicines for Hyperthyroidism: Antithyroid medicines cause your thyroid gland to make less thyroid hormone.

Generic Name	Brand Name
methimazole	Tapazole
propylthiouracil	Propyl-Thyracil or PTU

Arachnoid Cysts: Arachnoid cysts are fluid-filled sacs that occur on the arachnoid membrane that covers the brain (intracranial) and the spinal cord (spinal).

Atrial Fibrillation: Atrial fibrillation is the most common type of irregular heartbeat (arrhythmia). Normally, the heart beats in a strong, steady rhythm. In atrial fibrillation, a problem with the heart's electrical system causes the two upper parts of the heart, the atria, to quiver, or fibrillate.

Atrial Septal Defects: Atrial septal defects (ASDs) are a group of rare disorders of the heart that are present at birth (congenital) and involve a hole in the wall (septum) that separates the two upper-chambers (atria) of the heart.

B

Beta-Blockers for Atrial Fibrillation: Beta-blockers are rate-control medicines used for atrial fibrillation. They are used if your heart rate is too fast, which may cause symptoms.

Generic Name	Brand Name
acebutolol	Sectral
atenolol	Tenormin
carvedilol	Coreg
metoprolol	Lopressor, Toprol
nadolol	Corgard
propranolol	Inderal

Blood Thinners for Heart Failure Causes: If you are at risk for developing a blood clot in your heart, you might take a blood thinning medicine, also called an anticoagulant.

Blood Transfusion: Blood transfusion is a medical treatment that replaces blood lost through injury, surgery, or disease. The blood goes through a tube from a bag to an intravenous (IV) catheter and into your vein.

Breathing Problems: Using a Metered-Dose Inhaler: Diseases affecting the lungs—such as asthma, emphysema, chronic bronchitis, and chronic obstructive pulmonary disease (COPD)—share many of the same medicines. These medicines are often delivered through a metered-dose inhaler (MDI).

Bronchoscopy: Bronchoscopy is a procedure that allows your doctor to look at your airway through a thin viewing instrument called a bronchoscope. During a bronchoscopy, your doctor will examine your throat, larynx, trachea, and lower airways

C

Cannula: A hollow tube with a sharp, retractable inner core that can be inserted into a vein, an artery, or another body cavity.

Cardiac Catheterization: Cardiac catheterization is a test to check your heart. A cardiac catheterization can check blood flow in the coronary arteries, blood flow and blood pressure in the chambers of the heart, find out how well the heart valves work, and check for defects in the way the wall of the heart moves.

Caregiver:

Organizations

Family Caregiver Alliance

180 Montgomery Street

Suite 900

San Francisco, CA 94104

1-800-445-8106

Phone:

(415) 434-3388

Email: info@caregiver.org

Web Address: www.caregiver.org

This organization supports and assists people who are providing long-term care at home. It also provides education, research, services, and advocacy.

National Family Caregiver Support Program
U.S. Department of Health and Human Services
Suite Administration on Aging
Washington, DC 20201
Phone: (202) 401-4634
Fax: (202) 357-3555
Email: aoainfo@aoa.gov
Web Address: www.aoa.gov/AoARoot/AoA_Programs/HCLTC/
                Caregiver/index.aspx

Catheter Ablation for Atrial Fibrillation: If medicine is not effective or not tolerated for atrial fibrillation, a nonsurgical procedure called catheter ablation may be chosen. Catheter ablation for atrial fibrillation is relatively new and is still being studied. In this procedure thin, flexible wires are inserted into a vein in the groin and threaded up through the vein and into the heart. There is an electrode at the tip of the wires. The electrode sends out radio waves that create heat. This heat destroys the heart tissue that causes atrial fibrillation or the heart tissue that keeps it happening. Another option is to use freezing cold to destroy the heart tissue.

Chest X-Ray: A chest X-ray is a picture of the chest that shows your heart, lungs, airway, blood vessels, and lymph nodes. A chest X-ray also shows the bones of your spine and chest, including your breastbone, ribs, collarbone, and the upper part of your spine. A chest X-ray is the most common imaging test or X-ray used to find problems inside the chest.

Christmas Tree: Green connector to wall oxygen outlet.

Complete Blood Count (CBC): A complete blood count (CBC) gives important information about the kinds and numbers of cells in the blood, especially red blood cells, white blood cells, and platelets. A CBC helps your doctor check any symptoms, such as weakness, fatigue, or bruising, you may have. A CBC also helps him or her diagnose conditions, such as anemia, infection, and many other disorders.

Computed Tomography (CT) Scan of the Body: A computed tomography (CT) scan uses X-rays to make detailed pictures of structures inside of the body.

Cryosurgery: Treatment performed with an instrument that freezes and destroys abnormal tissue.

D

Diuretics for Congenital Heart Defects: Diuretics cause the kidneys to remove water and salt (sodium) from the body. This reduces the amount of fluid in the body and lowers blood pressure. Diuretics increase urination. So they are commonly called "water pills."

Generic Name	Brand Name
furosemide	Lasix
hydrochlorothiazide	Capozide
spironolactone	Aldactone

E

Echocardiogram: An echocardiogram (also called an echo) is a type of ultrasound test that uses high-pitched sound waves that are sent through a device called a transducer. The device picks up echoes of the sound waves as they bounce off the different parts of your heart. These echoes are turned into moving pictures of your heart that can be seen on a video screen.

Electrocardiogram: An ambulatory electrocardiogram (EKG or ECG) records the electrical activity of your heart while you do your usual activities. (Ambulatory means that you are able to walk.) Ambulatory monitors are referred to by several names, including ambulatory electrocardiogram, ambulatory EKG, Holter monitoring, 24-hour EKG, or cardiac event monitoring.

Electrical Cardioversion for Atrial Fibrillation: Electrical cardioversion is a procedure in which an electric current is used to reset the heart's rhythm back to its regular pattern (normal sinus rhythm). The low-voltage electric current enters the body through metal paddles or patches applied to the chest wall.

End of Life Issues: You will face many hard decisions as you near the end of life. Those decisions will include what kind of care you'd like to receive, where you'd like to receive care, and who will make decisions about your care should you not be able to make decisions yourself.

Endocarditis: Endocarditis is an infection of the heart's valves or its inner lining (endocardium). It is most common in people who have a damaged, diseased, or artificial heart valve.

Essential (Familial) Tremors: Tremor is an involuntary shaking movement that is repeated over and over. Although it may affect any part of the body, tremor most often affects the hands and head. Your voice may also shake. Sometimes the feet or torso may also shake. Essential tremor, which sometimes runs in families, is one of the most common types of tremor. It is shaking that is most noticeable when you are doing something like lifting a cup or pointing at an object.

F

Fainting: Fainting is a sudden, brief loss of consciousness. When people faint, or pass out, they usually fall down. After they are lying down, most people will recover quickly.

G

Gallbladder Scan: A gallbladder scan is a nuclear scanning test that is done to check gallbladder function. The scan can find blockage in the tubes (bile ducts) that lead from the liver to the gallbladder and small intestine (duodenum). See a picture of the gallbladder and the duodenum.

H

Healthcare-Associated Pneumonia: Healthcare-associated pneumonia (nosocomial pneumonia) is pneumonia that you get when you are in a hospital or nursing home.

High Potassium: Hyperkalemia is a condition caused by an abnormally high concentration of potassium in the blood. Potassium is a key element in contraction of muscles (including the heart) and for the functioning of many complicated proteins (enzymes). Potassium is found primarily in the skeletal muscle and bone, and participates with sodium to contribute to the normal flow between the body fluids and the cells of the body (homeostasis).

Hospice Care: Hospice care provides medical services, emotional support, and spiritual resources for people who are in the last stages of a serious illness, such as cancer or heart failure. Hospice care also helps family members manage the practical details and emotional challenges of caring for a dying loved one.

Hospital Discharge Planning: Discharge planning helps to make sure that you leave the hospital safely and smoothly and get the right care after that. You, the person who is caring for you, and your discharge planner work together to address your concerns in a discharge plan. Whether you go home, to a relative's home, to a rehabilitation facility, or to another health care setting, your plan outlines the care you need.

I

Incision Care After Surgery: After surgery, you will need to take care of the incision as it heals. Doing so may limit scarring, may help you avoid pain or discomfort, and may help lower the risk of problems like infection. Your doctor used either stitches, staples, tissue glue, or tape strips to close the incision. And you will need to keep the area clean, change the dressing according to your doctor's instructions, and watch for signs of infection.

Iron Deficiency Anemia: Iron deficiency anemia occurs when your body doesn't have enough iron.

J

J-PEG: Feeding tube inserted into stomach through skin/stomach wall.

K

L

Lab Test Results: Lab test results usually contain some type of unit of measurement. The units provide a way to report results so that they can be compared.

M

Meter dose Inhaler (MDI): An inhaler is a handheld device that delivers medicine in a measured dose while a person inhales. Inhalers are used in respiratory conditions such as asthma and chronic obstructive pulmonary disease (COPD). Inhaled medicine may work faster than oral medicines to relieve symptoms such as wheezing and spasms in the bronchial tubes, because the inhaler allows the medicine to go directly to the lungs. Inhaled medicine usually causes fewer side effects than oral medicine.

N

Nasogastric tube (NG Tube): A tube that is passed through the nose and down through the nasopharynx and esophagus into the stomach. It is a flexible tube made of rubber or plastic, and it has bidirectional potential. It can be used to remove the contents of the stomach, including air, to decompress the stomach, or to remove small solid objects and fluid, such as poison, from the stomach. An NG tube can also be used to put substances into the stomach, and so it may be used to place nutrients directly into the stomach when a patient cannot take food or drink by mouth.

Nurse practitioner (NP): A registered nurse (RN) who has completed an advanced training program in a medical specialty, such as pediatric care. An NP may be a primary, direct health care provider, and can prescribe medications.

Nurse, licensed practical (LPN): A nurse who has completed a 1- or 2-year training program in health care and has earned a state license. LPNs provide direct patient care for people with chronic illness, in nursing homes, hospitals, and home health care settings. They assist RNs in caring for acutely ill patients.

Nurse, licensed vocational (LVN): A nurse who has completed a one- or two-year training program in health care and earned a state license. LVNs provide direct patient care for people with chronic illness, in nursing homes, hospitals, and home settings. They assist RNs in caring for acutely ill patients.

Nurse, registered (RN): A nurse who has completed a 2- to 4-year degree program in nursing. Abbreviated. RNs provide direct patient care for acutely or chronically ill patients. RNs may further specialize in a particular area. For example, psychiatric nurses are RNs with special training in working with mentally ill patients, and trauma nurses work with physicians and surgeons to help patients in the emergency room of a hospital.

Nursing home: A residential facility for people with chronic illness or disability, particularly older people who have mobility and eating problems. Also known as a convalescent home and long-term care facility.

O

Open heart surgery: Surgery in which the chest is opened and surgery is performed on the heart. The term "open" refers to the chest, not to the heart itself. The heart may or may not be opened depending on the particular type of surgery.

Organ failure: The failure of an essential system in the body. Multiple organ failure is the failure of two or more systems, such as the cardiovascular, and renal systems, and is a common consequence of sepsis (the presence of bacteria in the bloods) and of shock (very low blood pressure).

Oxygen: The odorless gas that is present in the air and necessary to maintain life. Oxygen may be given in a medical setting, either to reduce the volume of other gases in the blood or as a vehicle for delivering anesthetics in gas form. It can be delivered via nasal tubes, an oxygen mask, or an oxygen tent. Patients with lung disease or damage may need to use portable oxygen devices on a temporary or permanent basis.

P

Pain management: The process of providing medical care that alleviates or reduces pain.

Palliative care: Medical or comfort care that reduces the severity of a disease or slows its progress, but does not provide a cure.

Pancreatitis: Inflammation of the pancreas. Of the many causes of pancreatitis, the most common are alcohol consumption and gallstones.

Penicillin: The most famous of all antibiotics, named for the fungal mold Penicillium notatum from which it is derived. Penicillin acts by destroying the cell wall of bacteria.

Pericarditis: Inflammation of the lining around the heart (the pericardium) that causes chest pain and accumulation of fluid around the heart (pericardial effusion). There are many causes of pericarditis, including infections, injury, radiation treatment, and chronic diseases.

Physician Assistant (PA): A PA is a mid-level medical practitioner who works under the supervision of a licensed doctor (an MD) or osteopathic physician (a DO).

Pharmacy: A location where prescription medications are sold. A pharmacy is constantly supervised by a licensed pharmacist.

Primary Care Provider (PCP): In insurance parlance, a physician who is chosen by or assigned to a patient and both provides primary care and acts as a gatekeeper to control access to other medical services.

Probiotics: live microorganisms (usually bacteria) that are similar to beneficial microorganisms found in the human gut that are taken as dietary supplements or found in foods.

Prognosis: The forecast of the probable outcome or course of a disease; the patient's chance of 'recovery'.

Pseudomonas infection: Infection usually with Pseudomonas aeruginosa, the versatile "blue-green pus bacteria" that opportunistically infects people, especially those who are immunocompromised.

Pulmonary: Having to do with the lungs.

Pulse: The rhythmic dilation of an artery that results from beating of the heart. Pulse is often measured by feeling the arteries of the wrist or neck.

Pump-oxygenator: A machine that does the work both of the heart (pump blood) and the lungs (oxygenate the blood). Used, for example, in open heart surgery. Blood returning to the heart is diverted through the machine before returning it to the arterial circulation. Also called a heart-lung machine.

Q

R

Radiology: The medical specialty concerned with radiation for the diagnosis and treatment of disease, including both ionizing radiation such as X-rays and nonionizing radiation such as ultrasound.

Rate, heart (HR): Number of heart beats per minute. The normal resting adult heart beats regularly at an average rate of 60 times per minute.

Red blood cell: The blood cell that carries oxygen. Red cells contain hemoglobin and it is the hemoglobin which permits them to transport oxygen (and carbon dioxide).

Reflux: The term used when liquid backs up into the esophagus from the stomach.

Rehabilitation: The process of helping a person who has suffered an illness or injury restore lost skills and so regain maximum self-sufficiency.

Renal: Having to do with the kidney.

Respiratory: Having to do with respiration.

Respiratory distress syndrome, acute (ARDS): Respiratory failure of sudden onset due to fluid in the lungs (pulmonary edema), following an abrupt increase in the permeability of the normal barrier between the capillaries in the lungs and the air sacs.

Respiratory failure: Inability of the lungs to perform their basic task of gas exchange, the transfer of oxygen from inhaled air into the blood and the transfer of carbon dioxide from the blood into exhaled air.

Respiratory rate: The number of breaths per minute or, more formally, the number of movements indicative of inspiration and expiration per unit time.

Resuscitate: To restore to life. Derived from the Latin resuscitare, to reawaken.

Rh factor: An antigen found on the surface of red blood cells. Red blood cells with the antigen are said to be Rh positive (Rh+). Those without the surface antigen are said to be Rh negative (Rh-).

Rhythm, sinus: The normal regular rhythm of the heart set by the natural pacemaker of the heart called the sinoatrial (or sinus) node. It is located in the wall of the right atrium (the right upper chamber of the heart).

Right atrium: The right upper chamber of the heart. The right atrium receives deoxygenated blood from the body through the vena cava and pumps it into the right ventricle which then sends it to the lungs to be oxygenated.

Right ventricle: The lower right chamber of the heart that receives deoxygenated blood from the right atrium and pumps it under low pressure into the lungs via the pulmonary artery.

S

Scan, CAT: Pictures of structures within the body created by a computer that takes the data from multiple X-ray images and turns them in pictures. The CAT (computerized axial tomography) scan can reveal some soft-tissue and other structures that cannot be seen in conventional X-rays. Using the same dosage of radiation as that of an ordinary X-ray machine, an entire slice of the body can be made visible with about 100 times more clarity with the CAT scan.

Secondary amyloidosis: One of a group of diseases (called amyloidosis) in which protein deposits (amyloid) accumulate in one or more organ systems in the body.

Sedative: A drug that calms a patient, easing agitation and permitting sleep.

Sepsis: The presence of bacteria (bacteremia), other infectious organisms, or toxins created by infectious organisms in the bloodstream with spread throughout the body.

Septum, atrial: The wall between the right and left atria (the upper chambers) of the heart.

Septum, ventricular: The wall between the two lower chambers (ventricles) of the heart.

Shortness of breath: Difficulty in breathing. Medically referred to as dyspnea. Shortness of breath can be caused by respiratory (breathing passages and lungs) or circulatory (heart and blood vessels) conditions and other conditions such as severe anemia or high fever.

Sinus bradycardia: A regular but unusually slow heart beat (50 beats/ minute or less at rest). Sinus bradycardia can be the result of many things including good physical fitness, medications, and some forms of heart block.

Sinus tachycardia: Fast heartbeat (tachycardia) that occurs because of overly rapid firing by the sinoatrial node. Sinus tachycardia is usually a rapid contraction of a normal heart in response to a condition, drug, or disease. In some cases sinus tachycardia can be a sign of heart failure, heart valve disease, or other illness.

STAT: A common medical abbreviation for urgent or rush.

Sternum: The long flat bone in the upper middle of the front of the chest. The sternum articulates (comes together) with the cartilages of the first seven ribs and with the clavicle (collarbone) on either side.

Streptococcus: A group of bacteria that causes a multitude of diseases. Under a microscope, streptococcus bacteria look like a twisted bunch of round berries. Illnesses caused by streptococcus include strep throat, strep pneumonia, scarlet fever, rheumatic fever (and rheumatic heart valve damage).

Sulfonamides: The sulfa-related group of antibiotics, which are used to treat bacterial infection and some fungal infections.

Syncope: Partial or complete loss of consciousness with interruption of awareness of oneself and ones surroundings. When the loss of consciousness is temporary and there is spontaneous recovery, it is referred to as syncope or, in nonmedical quarters, fainting.

Systole: The time period when the heart is contracting. The period specifically during which the left ventricle of the heart contracts.

T

Tachycardia, ventricular: An abnormally rapid heart rhythm that originates from a ventricle, one of the lower chambers of the heart.

Although the beat is regular, ventricular tachycardia is life-threatening because it can lead to a dreaded condition, ventricular fibrillation.

Tracheostomy: Surgery to create an opening (stoma) into the windpipe. The opening itself may also be called a tracheostomy. A tracheostomy may be made as an emergency measure if the airway is blocked.

Therapy, respiratory: Exercises and treatments designed to help patients maintain and recover lung function, such as with cystic fibrosis and after surgery.

Thoracic: Pertaining to the chest. For example, the thoracic aorta is the part of the aorta that lies within the chest.

Thrush: Yeast infection of the mouth and throat, characterized by patches of white, caused by the fungus Candida albicans.

Transfusion: The transfer of blood or blood products from one person (the donor) into the bloodstream of another person (the recipient). In most situations, transfusion is done as a lifesaving maneuver to replace blood cells or blood products lost through severe bleeding.

Trauma: A physical or emotional injury.

U

Ultrasound: High-frequency sound waves. Ultra-sound waves can be bounced off tissues by using special devices. The echoes are then converted into a picture called a sonogram. Ultrasound imaging allows an inside view of soft tissues and body cavities without the use of invasive techniques.

V

Valve, Mitral: One of the four valves of the heart, the mitral valve is situated between the left atrium and the left ventricle. It permits blood to flow one way: from the left atrium into the left ventricle. The mitral valve has two flaps (cusps) and so is called "mitral" because it looks like a bishop's miter or headdress. Also known as the bicuspid valve.

Venous, Central Catheter (Central Line): A catheter (tube) that is passed through a vein to end up in the thoracic (chest) portion of the vena cava (the large vein returning blood to the heart) or in the right atrium of the heart.

Ventricular Septal Defects: Ventricular septal defects are heart defects that are present at birth (congenital). The normal heart has four chambers. The two upper chambers, known as atria, are separated from each other by a fibrous partition known as the atrial septum. The two lower chambers are known as ventricles and are separated from each other by the ventricular septum. Valves connect the atria (left and right) to their respective ventricles. The aorta, the main vessel of arterial circulation, carries blood from the left ventricle and away from the heart.

W

Warfarin: An anticoagulant drug (brand names: Coumarin, Panwarfin, Sofarin) taken to prevent the blood from clotting and to treat blood clots and overly thick blood.

White blood cell: One of the cells the body makes to help fight infections. There are several types of white blood cells (leukocytes).

X

X-ray: High-energy radiation with waves shorter than those of visible light. X-ray is used in low doses to make images that help to diagnose diseases and in high doses to treat cancer.

Xanax: is used for the treatment of anxiety disorders and panic attacks. Anxiety disorders are characterized by unrealistic worry and apprehension, causing symptoms of restlessness, aches, trembling, shortness of breath, smothering sensation, palpitations, sweating, cold clammy hands, lightheadedness, flushing, exaggerated startle responses, problems concentrating, and insomnia.

Y

Z

ENDNOTES

1   Republic, Plato. *Translated by G.M.A. Grube/C.D.C. Reeve 2nd Edition*. IN: Hackett Publishing Company, 1992. Pp 211-212.

2   Confraternity of Christian Doctrine. *Saint Joseph Edition of the New American Bible*. NY: Catholic Publishing Company, 1992. JB 7: 1-4, 6-7

3   Confraternity of Christian Doctrine. *Saint Joseph Edition of the New American Bible*. NY: Catholic Publishing Company, 1992. MT 11:30

4   Confraternity of Christian Doctrine. *Saint Joseph Edition of the New American Bible*. NY: Catholic Publishing Company, 1992. EPH 5: 25-32.

5   Bishop's Conference on the Liturgy. National Conference of Catholic Bishops. *The Roman Ritual. The Rite of Marriage*. New Jersey. Catholic Book Publishing Corp. 1970. Consent. Pg 13.

6   http://radiopaedia.org/articles/pulmonary-mycobacterium-avium-complex-infection . Accessed December 5, 2014

7   http://www.cdc.gov/ncidod/dbmd/diseaseinfo/mycobacteriumavium_t.htm. Accessed December 5, 2014.

8   http://emedicine.medscape.com/article/222664-treatment . Accessed December 8, 2014.

9   http://www.lung.org/lung-disease/bronchiectasis/ . Accessed December 8, 2014

10   http://www.webmd.com/a-to-z-guides/pseudomonas-infection-topic-overview . Accessed December 8, 2014

11   http://www.medicinenet.com/atrial_fibrillation_pictures_slideshow/article.htm . Accessed December 15, 2014.

12   ibid

13 ibid

14 http://www.mayoclinic.org/diseases-conditions/endocarditis/basics/definition/con-20022403

15 Confraternity of Christian Doctrine. *Saint Joseph Edition of the New American Bible*. NY: Catholic Publishing Company, 1992. 1 COR 13:13.

16 Confraternity of Christian Doctrine. *Saint Joseph Edition of the New American Bible*. NY: Catholic Publishing Company, 1992. Mk 9:24.

17 http://lyrics.wikia.com/B.B._King:Born_Again_Human. Accessed February 27, 2015.

18 http://en.wikipedia.org/wiki/Human_Touch. Accessed February 27, 2015.

19 http://en.wikipedia.org/wiki/The_Ever_Popular_Tortured_Artist_Effect. Accessed February 27, 2015.

20 http://www.ncbi.nlm.nih.gov/pmc/articles/PMC3264929/ . Accessed February 11, 2015.

21 Confraternity of Christian Doctrine. *Saint Joseph Edition of the New American Bible*. NY: Catholic Publishing Company, 1992. PS 147: 1-6.

22 Confraternity of Christian Doctrine. *Saint Joseph Edition of the New American Bible*. NY: Catholic Publishing Company, 1992. LK 2:19.

23 http://www.paulthorn.com/store/cd/clip/pimps/11-i_dont_like_half_the_folks_i_love.mp3. Accessed February 27, 2015

24 Confraternity of Christian Doctrine. *Saint Joseph Edition of the New American Bible*. NY: Catholic Publishing Company, 1992. MK 1: 29-39

25 Confraternity of Christian Doctrine. *Saint Joseph Edition of the New American Bible*. NY: Catholic Publishing Company, 1992. MT 7:14.

26 Pope Paul VI, *On Evangelization in the Modern World: EVANGELII NUNTIANDI. Apostolic Exhortation. December 8, 1975. (para 21)*.

27 Charles de Foucauld, Antier Jan-Jacques, Ignatius Press, 1999.

28 Confraternity of Christian Doctrine. *Saint Joseph Edition of the New American Bible*. NY: Catholic Publishing Company, 1992. MK 12: 30-31.

29 Confraternity of Christian Doctrine. *Saint Joseph Edition of the New American Bible*. NY: Catholic Publishing Company, 1992. MT 5:12

30   Confraternity of Christian Doctrine. *Saint Joseph Edition of the New American Bible*. NY: Catholic Publishing Company, 1992. MT 28: 18-20.

31   Confraternity of Christian Doctrine. *Saint Joseph Edition of the New American Bible*. NY: Catholic Publishing Company, 1992. MT 14:31.

32   Confraternity of Christian Doctrine. *Saint Joseph Edition of the New American Bible*. NY: Catholic Publishing Company, 1992. MK 9:24.

33   Confraternity of Christian Doctrine. *Saint Joseph Edition of the New American Bible*. NY: Catholic Publishing Company, 1992. JN 6:20.

CPSIA information can be obtained
at www.ICGtesting.com
Printed in the USA
FSOW04n1353030815
9469FS